CHANGE YOUR
CHOICES
CHANGE YOUR
LIFE

LOWELL K. OSWALD, PhD
AND JOHN WATERBURY, LPC

PLAIN SIGHT PUBLISHING
AN IMPRINT OF CEDAR FORT, INC.
SPRINGVILLE, UTAH

ISBN 13: 978-1-4621-1073-5

Published by Plain Sight Publishing, an imprint of Cedar Fort, Inc.
2373 W. 700 S., Springville, UT 84663
Distributed by Cedar Fort, Inc., www.cedarfort.com

LIBRARY OF CONGRESS CATALOGING-IN-PUBLICATION DATA

Oswald, Lowell K. (Lowell Keith), author.
Change your choices, change your life : discovering your path to emotional healing and spiritual growth / Lowell K. Oswald, PhD and John Waterbury, LPC.
    pages cm
Includes bibliographical references and index.
Summary: Discusses the characteristics and realities of long-term emotional damage caused by abuse and offers hope and healing for overcoming past pain.
ISBN 978-1-4621-1073-5 (alk. paper)
 1. Psychological abuse victims--Rehabilitation. 2. Psychological abuse victims--Religious life. 3. Psychological abuse--Religious aspects--Christianity.
 I. Waterbury, John, 1949-, author. II. Title.

BV4596.P87O89 2012
248.8'6--dc23

2012035013

Cover design by Erica Dixon
Cover design © 2012 by Lyle Mortimer
Edited and typeset by Whitney A. Lindsley

Printed in the United States of America

10 9 8 7 6 5 4 3 2 1

To our wives, Laurie and Melinda,
for their encouragement, faith,
and patience

PRAISE FOR
CHANGE YOUR CHOICES, CHANGE YOUR LIFE

Change Your Choices, Change Your Life can be profoundly helpful to anyone suffering from abuse. In addition, the messages in this book offer solutions to all who face challenges in their life. Dr. Oswald's personal experiences led him to develop the process that can help many others reach into their souls and find relief.

GARY AND JOY LUNDBERG
Authors of I Don't Have to Make Everything All Better

For those searching for healing from the effects of abuse or mental illness this book will engender a desire to go to battle for a more fulfilling life. As the authors emphasize, "Life is about choosing . . . not just having choices." The personal experiences shared in this beautiful book illustrate the central paradox that the battle is best fought from a submissive attitude to God's will.

JENNIFER CARDINAL, PhD
Licensed Psychologist

Authors Lowell K. Oswald and John Waterbury take us on a compelling journey of emergence from suffering, self-doubt, and hopelessness to change . . . The authors systematically outline the steps to wellness and transformation by presenting tools emphasizing our ability to make the choice to recognize, process, and change patterns of self-defeating perceptions and behavior. As a clinical mental health therapist, I see this book as a valuable tool for both professionals and clients.

ALICE WYNN, LPC, NCC
Director, Sunrise Therapy, LLC

CONTENTS

A NOTE TO THE READER

CHANGE YOUR CHOICES, CHANGE YOUR LIFE DESCRIBES life lessons learned by Lowell Oswald as he struggled to overcome the effects of his past. These lessons are included at the beginning of each chapter. Within each chapter, under the heading of "Clinical Insights," John Waterbury shares life-management skills and guiding principles for individuals working through the recovery process. The book promotes a new beginning by clarifying correct principles and by inspiring hope for those who are striving to overcome unhealthy patterns of behavior and desiring to experience greater happiness.

The authors of the book use terms such as *abuse, anxiety* or *anxiety disorders, depression, dysfunctional* or *troubled family*, and *unhealthy patterns of behavior* to describe influences that may interfere with our ability to heal emotionally and grow spiritually. These terms are defined below:

ABUSE

Abuse is defined as anything that is harmful, injurious, or offensive. It is a pattern of behavior in which physical violence or emotional coercion, or both, are used to gain or maintain power or control in a relationship. There are several major types of abuse: physical, verbal, emotional, or sexual abuse of a child or an adult.

Federal health officials report, "Almost 60% of American adults say they had difficult childhoods featuring abusive or troubled family members or parents who were absent due to separation or divorce." Furthermore, "Nearly 9% said that while growing up they underwent five or more 'adverse childhood experiences' ranging from verbal, physical or sexual abuse to family dysfunction such as domestic violence, drug or alcohol abuse, or the absence of a parent."[1]

ANXIETY DISORDERS

The National Institute of Mental Health (NIMH) reports that anxiety disorders affect about forty million American adults every year, causing them to be filled with fearfulness and uncertainty. Unlike the relatively mild, brief anxiety caused by a stressful event (such as speaking in public or a first date), anxiety disorders last at least six months and can increase in severity if not treated. Anxiety disorders commonly occur along with other mental or physical illnesses, including alcohol or substance abuse, which may mask anxiety symptoms or make them worse. In some cases, these other illnesses must be treated before a person will respond to treatment for the anxiety disorder.

Anxiety disorders include such conditions as panic disorder, obsessive-compulsive disorder (OCD), post-traumatic stress disorder (PTSD), social anxiety disorder, specific phobias, and generalized anxiety disorder (GAD). Effective therapies for anxiety disorders are available, and research is uncovering new treatments that can help most people with anxiety disorders lead productive, fulfilling lives. If you think you have an anxiety disorder, you should seek professional treatment.

DEPRESSION

According to the NIMH, from time to time, everyone feels blue or sad, but these feelings are usually temporary and pass within a couple of days. When a person has a depressive disorder, it interferes with daily life, inhibits normal functioning, and causes pain for both the person with the disorder and family members. Depression is a common but serious illness, and most individuals who experience it need treatment to improve.

There are several types of depressive disorders. The most common are major depressive disorder (which affects over a million American adults, in a given year) and dysthymic disorder. Other forms of depression include bipolar disorder, psychotic depression, postpartum depression, and seasonal affective disorder (SAD).

Many people with depression never seek help. However, even those with the most severe depression can improve with treatment. Extensive research has resulted in the development of medications, psychotherapies, and other methods designed to treat individuals with this disabling disorder. If you think you have a depressive disorder, you should seek professional treatment.

TROUBLED FAMILY

Most families experience periods of time during which functioning is impaired by stressful circumstances. Healthy families usually return to normal functioning once the challenging situation is over. In troubled families, problems tend to be chronic and children's emotional needs are rarely met. As a result, a variety of unhealthy patterns of behavior may develop.

UNHEALTHY PATTERNS OF BEHAVIOR

Unhealthy patterns of behavior are actions that prevent us from healing emotionally and growing spiritually. They may include, but are not limited to, addictions (alcohol, drugs, smoking, gambling, food, video games, television, pornography, sex, shopping, work, hoarding, and so on), anger management problems, perfectionism, religious zealotry, and destructive relationships.

NOTES

1. Steven Reinberg, "CDC: Majority of U.S. adults had troubled childhoods," accessed December 17, 2011, http://www.usatoday.com/your-life/parenting-family/2010-12-17-adult-majority-troubled-childhood_N.htm.

INTRODUCTION

MY TEN SIBLINGS AND I GREW UP IN A TROUBLED family. Unfortunately, my story is not a singular one. Many others have suffered from some sort of abuse, mental illness, or other persistent life challenge. You may have struggled, know others who have struggled, or may still be struggling as a result of such experiences.

Change Your Choices, Change Your Life identifies ways to heal emotionally and grow spiritually. We discover that God, caring individuals, and appropriate professional support can help those who silently suffer. Together we can learn how to replace fear and despair with love and hope as we humble ourselves, exercise faith and patience, and submit to God's will.

Hope is available for those struggling to overcome unhealthy patterns of behavior. As we follow a path that includes obedience to God and seek out and obtain support from caring individuals, we discover we are not alone in our struggles. We will come to know that a loving God is mindful of our needs. And in his own way and time, he will lighten our burdens and lift us out of the darkness of fear and despair and into the glorious light of truth, where we will better know correct principles and understand things as they really are.

Our unhealthy, if not destructive, patterns of behavior may have come directly from severe abuse, the biochemical effects of untreated or partially treated mental illness, or perhaps some other persistent life challenge. Nevertheless, God will deliver us from the bondage of these behaviors if we put our trust in him.

Most of us are familiar with the story about a man who was at his house when heavy rains poured down, the river crested, and the town flooded. As he stood on his front porch, the neighborhood completely under water, two men came by in a rowboat. "Can we take you to safety?" one called out. The man shook his head. "No, thank you. I have faith in God, and he will save me."

A little later, the waters had risen and the man was on the roof of his porch when several other people happened along in a motorboat. "Say, there, would you like to come with us?" one of them called. "No, thank you," the man replied. "I have faith in God, and he will save me."

The waters continued to rise with alarming speed, and the man soon found himself on the roof of his house. A helicopter came by and hovered overhead as the pilot broadcasted, "Let me drop a line and get you out of there."

"No, thank you," the man called back. "I have faith in God, and he will save me."

The man perished in the flood and went to heaven, where he was met at the Pearly Gates by Saint Peter. Extremely saddened and upset, the man requested to talk to God. His request was granted.

"Heavenly Father," the man cried, "I had faith in you to save me from the flood, and you didn't come through for me!" Astonished, God replied, "What are you talking about? I sent you two boats and a helicopter!"[1]

Faith in God is an active rather than a passive process. It requires effort. True faith is based upon an understanding of correct principles. It's much more than the mere belief that he exists. Such faith generally motivates us to take physical and mental action and to choose to actively pursue that which is hoped for in order to receive help.

CLINICAL INSIGHTS

The principles of the scriptures are true. Unfortunately, when we're overwhelmed by guilt, shame, depression, anxiety disorders, or life itself, those same principles may seem impossible to live. While they are correct, they may seem beyond our reach because of our imperfect perception.

It's the old "you-can't-get-there-from-here" concept. When we believe we are too far gone to progress, the doctrines of the world tend to reinforce that belief, making it extremely difficult to break the pattern.

That is the beauty of God's plan. When we believe our imperfections stop us from reaching him, when the distance seems too great, when we lose hope of finding our way home, he consistently finds a way to come to us. Not just sometimes, and not just for those who appear to be doing all of the right things, but for all of us, whenever we're ready.

The purpose of this book is to help facilitate emotional healing and spiritual growth—a point of departure from old ideas, ways, and patterns of behavior that are no longer productive. This book's purpose is to help promote a new direction in life by clarifying correct principles and inspiring hope. We know that there is no end to learning, no end to growth, and no way to fail unless we misunderstand eternal principles.

It's easy to feel lost in this world. With the challenges of abuse, depression, and anxiety disorders, and with what appears to be an endless array of temptations and painful situations, we are pushed to what feels beyond our limits. At such times, it may even be difficult to take comfort in the following scripture: "God is faithful, who will not suffer you to be tempted above that ye are able; but will with the temptation also make a way to escape, that ye may be able to bear it" (1 Corinthians 10:13).

Fortunately, and usually without our awareness, this type of emotional and spiritual Gethsemane plays a significant role in our lives. It acts as a necessary, but often frustrating, process that forces us to reexamine and redefine who we really are. The confusion and bewilderment we feel may serve to overwhelm us temporarily, but eventually we are compelled to see ourselves more clearly and to identify the hidden patterns and purposes in life.

Except for eternal principles, everything in life has a beginning, a middle, and an end—the good times and the bad, the happy and the sad. This is the way it's intended to be. Nothing remains the same. Everything is always in a state of transition from the beginning to the end. This process repeats itself and provides us with opportunities to grow spiritually.

Despite how unfair or unfortunate or unappealing we may perceive our lives to be, each hardship will eventually pass. And as the result of these natural laws, our perception will be altered and we will begin to see things as they really are. We discover that happiness is not a final destination but that it is a journey during which we learn what matters in life. Throughout this journey, we experience periods of pain, suffering, and sorrow as well as happiness, joy, and peace.

NOTES

1.   Laura's Inspirational Pages, "What is God's role? What is ours?" accessed January 2, 2012, http://lpintop.tripod.com/laurasinspirationalpages/id3.html.

PART ONE

HEALING EMOTIONALLY

CHAPTER 1

THE HEALING PROCESS

UCCESSFULLY LIVING THE CHRISTIAN LIFE MAY BE especially challenging for those who have experienced some form of abuse. Giving in to a parent, sibling, spouse, or any other individual in an abusive situation creates an assortment of negative, demeaning, and lifeless conditions, and the idea of submitting to a heavenly being becomes counterintuitive.

In any type of controlling relationship, submitting—or being forced into submission—means temporarily giving up your agency, not your will. It's your will that helps you to survive. Love, trust, and hope are feelings that are manipulated; these feelings are eventually replaced with hate, mistrust, anxiety, and fear—survival responses we naturally resort to in order to endure painful times.

In our home, physical and emotional abuse was a regular part of our normal daily life. Shame, guilt, humiliation, and physical intimidation were used to control our behavior and force us into submission. My siblings and I vividly remember the chaos, which included

- Sitting through frequent late-night arguments between our parents.

- Watching our father strike our mother with his fist when she disagreed with him

1

- Reassuring our father, after a long fight, that we really loved him, that we would obey him, and that the person he had targeted would do better next time.

- Trying to analyze each nightly argument and coming up with a new and acceptable solution for our father, which he promptly ignored, while he waited for the target of his anger to submit to his will.

- Watching our father make life miserable for a sibling just hours or days before a big event in their lives like a date, school play, or sporting event.

- Watching his personality completely change when he was around other people as opposed to when he was at home with family members.

- Listening to our father frequently threaten divorce in an attempt to exert control over our mother.

- Watching him slowly load a gun, put it to his head, and shout at family members, "Is this really what you want?"

- Fearing and experiencing the wrath of our father if we broke an item in the house.

- Having the police come to our house because of our father's out-of-control behavior.

- Being yelled at or punished for laughing.

- Seeing a sibling get physically injured by our father during an argument and experiencing the chaos that followed.

- Trying to keep our house clean, which usually resulted in our father engaging in angry tirades because some small, worthless item was misplaced or discarded.

- Frequently hearing our father ask our mother how she will feed their children and where they will live if he leaves or kills himself.

My intense desire to be different from my father—to one day have my own family and to be a loving husband and father—helped me endure those painful times. While my father was successful during my childhood at controlling my God-given agency, he could not take away my will to become what God wanted me to be—happy, loving, and free from the bondage of constantly feeling anxiety and fear.

I need to draw a distinction between the terms agency and will. They are not the same. Agency is the privilege of choice. Will is a deliberate choice and "the power to arrive at one's own decision and to act upon it independently in spite of opposition."[1] Agency is what God gives us. He is the author of choice. Will is what we choose to give God. It takes great faith to submit our will to God's.

In submitting to God's will, we are gaining our agency, not losing it. This is a beautiful paradox. The marvelous blessings of Christ's teachings and atonement are that they enable us to manage and overcome the effects of abuse and other unhealthy patterns of behavior. Jesus Christ willingly made the ultimate sacrifice because of his great love for each of us. Once we experience this love, we begin to understand that submitting to God's will is the only way to find real joy and happiness. Our lives take on new meaning and we see the world through different eyes. We have an increased desire to do God's will, knowing that through submissiveness and humility, we can truly experience his love—a perfect love that changes our hearts, fills us with joy, and gives us the energy and the desire to pursue better lives.

God will never force us to change. He will guide and direct us, and even send others into our lives to assist us, but will always honor our privilege of choice. We alone have the power to choose our life and what we will become.

Hope motivates us to change and helps us begin to heal. We can strengthen our hope as we actively strive to understand and do God's will. When we have faith in and hope of God's ability to bless us, he is able to communicate his will and we discover, as his children, that he has the power to heal us.

CLINICAL INSIGHTS

OVERCOMING UNHEALTHY
PATTERNS OF BEHAVIOR

Since some of the basic concepts of Christian religions are obedience, sacrifice, service, and loving those around us in spite of their mistakes, we tend to get confused about limits, boundaries, tolerance, and endurance. When we add to this foundation the concept that pain is an unavoidable and yet necessary part of our experience in this world, we tend to think that we're supposed to quietly endure this pain. We are taught to endure to the end, but we often misunderstand the importance of enduring well or enjoying the process along the way. As a result, the pain caused by people and circumstances often push us beyond our limits.

When we feel confusion and guilt about the necessity of meeting our needs and exercising our rights, we cannot develop healthy boundaries for ourselves. These uncertain boundaries often lead to our being used, abused, and confused. As our confusion continues, we eventually convert it to anger—anger at ourselves, at our families, and even at God. All of these dynamics result from misunderstanding and misperceiving correct principles.

In reality, while pain may be purposeful in spurring us on to higher levels, it was never meant to destroy. Unfortunately, many people are born into families where correct principles are never clearly understood. They may learn to survive but are seldom able to break the generational chains of dysfunction. Inadvertently they pass the incorrect principles on to the following generations in the form of dependency, poor self-image, impaired coping techniques, depression, anxiety disorders, and various types of abuse that negatively influence all areas of life.

Incorrect perceptions lead to thinking and behavioral patterns that result in an external locus of control. This is the process in which other people, situations, and circumstances become the controlling factors in our decision-making. This is the opposite of an internal locus of control that is defined as knowing who we are, being healthy enough to identify and meet our own needs, and being assertive enough to exercise our agency.

Unfortunately, this type of dysfunction impairs the laws of growth

4

and development. People from this type of family feel stuck. Their personal identities become enmeshed with unhealthy behaviors. To make reality manageable, they develop several types of denial. They begin to justify their conditions to provide a tolerable level of self-esteem and even begin to see the self-defeating behavioral patterns as an immutable part of their natures. They say things like, "That's just the way I've always been." With the resignation that results, they begin to believe that it's the way they will always be.

None of this is intentional. They simply don't know how to keep from doing what they're doing. It's what they were taught. It's all they know. When this type of dysfunction is generations deep, the afflicted individuals seem incapable of responding to guidance and direction from friends or church leaders. As a result of living in this state of confusion and helplessness, they no longer perceive things clearly, their ability to accurately interpret the severity of their situations diminishes, and the paralysis of spiritual, emotional, and physical lethargy sets in. At that point, living Christian principles seems beyond their limited capacity. So they survive and they endure. They become entrapped by solutions that don't solve their problems and are ostracized by neighbors, coworkers, and clergy who don't understand.

These patterns of unhealthy behavior cause pain, confusion, and distress to both the individual and the individual's family. At first glance, the individual assumes that such thoughts, feelings, and habits apply to everyone. In reality, the patterns of dysfunction that clearly define the problem differ from healthy behavioral patterns in three specific areas:

1. *Frequency.* This refers to the increased occurrence of specific, identifiable self-defeating behavioral patterns.

2. *Intensity.* Once these patterns develop, the devastation and severity clearly separate them from healthy patterns.

3. *Duration.* When these patterns are in place, they tend to perpetuate themselves, passing from generation to generation and leaving devastation in their wake.

These behavioral patterns are addictions. An addiction to such behavior refers to a much greater variety of dysfunction than merely addiction to alcohol or other drugs. It includes, but is not limited to, physical, sexual, verbal, and emotional abuse or neglect. It includes any type of dysfunctional family system that generates negative and self-limiting methods of coping with thoughts, feelings, and personal needs.

Since we, as human beings, tend to do what we think is in our best interest, it should not surprise us that victims in a dysfunctional family develop these behaviors in an attempt to survive the painful and threatening situations in their homes. The problem is that these behaviors make pain, confusion, and distress a way of life and form the basis of an unhealthy perception of reality.

These patterns of behavior cause confusion when an individual leaves the home. The survival techniques that have taken years to develop in the dysfunctional home, and which served effectively during the individual's development, no longer consistently produce acceptable levels of functioning, and the person is left in a quandary. Their tools and techniques don't work. Their self-esteem and confidence become impaired. Because these individuals received inconsistent messages in the dysfunctional home, they develop problems with trusting others. They ignore, deny, or repress their feelings to the point that they often don't feel anything. They tend to go overboard in relationships, giving extreme loyalty and dedication, even when these qualities are not justified. This often leads to depression and a pattern of failed relationships.

These individuals tend to be caretakers and attempt to rescue others. In other words, they feel responsible for other people, for their feelings, thoughts, choices, and well-being. They are generally attracted to people who are in the midst of personal problems. They become controlling—feeling almost compelled to solve the problems of others—and ultimately feel intense anxiety, pity, and guilt when they find they are unable to "fix" other people. They are generally very sensitive to the feelings of others and are able to anticipate their needs. Sooner or later, however, they begin to ask why others don't do the same for them, why no one seems sensitive to their needs, and why no one appreciates them. The answer seems to be that much of the advice they give out is unwanted, unappreciated, and unused. Their feelings are hurt, and they become angry and resentful.

In other cases they may take the opposite role, that of victim, leaving others to make their own life decisions and then becoming negative, critical, and depressed when things don't turn out the way they want. Unfortunately, these individuals often spend a major part of their lives locked into this type of self-defeating behavior, never understanding how it all could have happened in the first place.

In an effort to gain understanding, they may seek out self-help books and personal development courses. However, insight seldom develops during this active seeking phase because these individuals don't have the necessary foundation to accurately assess and assimilate what is happening in their lives. What they learn seems to contradict what they are used to practicing. It's extremely difficult for a person who is committed to an unhealthy and dysfunctional perception to be able to implement a healthy and functional behavioral system.

These individuals actually set themselves up for failure by trying to accommodate others. They find themselves saying yes when they really mean no. They end up doing things for others that they don't want to do. They lose sight of their own needs, convincing themselves that what they want and need is not really important. Much of their happiness is derived from trying to please everyone around them. This, of course, is impossible. Nevertheless, these individuals often become deeply involved in community causes, social movements, and civil rights activities. They are always fighting for the rights of others and always striving for the down-and-out. It's much easier for them to express anger about the injustices done to others than it is to focus on the injustices done to them.

They tend to be identified as giving people. In reality, these behaviors are chosen because these individuals feel safest when giving to others. When someone tries to do something for them, they often feel insecure and uncomfortable and have great difficulty accepting compliments.

Since their giving tendencies attract people with needy personalities, they find their lives filled with crises and lost causes. They seem willing to abandon their normal routine at the drop of a hat to respond to such causes. They overcommit themselves, feel pressured beyond their ability to cope, and eventually burn themselves out. Increased anxiety and panic attacks are common hazards associated with this lifestyle. Yet unless they are involved in such activities, they may feel bored, empty, and worthless.

On one hand, these people go overboard trying to help all the people around them. On the other hand, they resent the intense demands on their time. When this occurs, they blame others for making them crazy, angry, and victimized. They experience guilt for feeling this way and ask for forgiveness. In this manner, they become locked into a continuing series of self-defeating behaviors.

Even though it's clear that they come from dysfunctional families, most people from dysfunctional families will vehemently deny that their family was troubled. Because of their low self-worth, they tend to blame themselves for everything and are extremely critical of the way they think, feel, look, and act. When others blame or criticize them, they become angry, defensive, and self-righteous.

As they compare themselves to others, they often feel that they are different from the rest of the world and that they are never good enough, no matter what they do and how hard they try. This results in a tremendous amount of disabling guilt, which in turn makes it difficult for them to do anything fun or enjoyable for themselves.

Since many of these individuals have been the victims of sexual, physical, verbal, or emotional abuse, they often fear rejection or abandonment and tend to take on the role of a victim. They are afraid of making mistakes and set expectations for themselves so high that anything short of perfection is unacceptable. Their language and thoughts are full of "shoulds" and "should nots," and yet when they are faced with making decisions, they are incapable of doing so.

In an attempt to deal with all these feelings and contradictions, these individuals become depressed easily. The frequency, intensity, and duration of these periods of depression increase significantly over time. They wish good things would happen to them but don't actually believe that they will. They seem to feel that no matter what they do, they are undeserving and unsuccessful. Since they feel they are incapable of being loved, they tend to settle for simply being needed. As the dysfunction increases, they find that they fail even at this.

The only positive about such an unhealthy behavioral pattern is that it responds well to treatment. In a therapeutic setting designed especially for the unique combination of problems that characterize the illness, people with these problems find the support, direction, and hope that enable them to make the necessary changes in their lives. They learn to free themselves from the emotional shackles, obsessive thoughts, and self-defeating patterns of behavior that have imprisoned them. With new skills and effective self-development tools, they find themselves able to learn and develop in ways that lead to greater insight and to increased understanding, wisdom, and spirituality.

THE GIFTS OF CHEMICAL IMBALANCES

Rarely does anyone see anything 100 percent accurately, and, because of this, we often miss the positive lessons in life when we only focus on the negative aspects of our situations and circumstances. When this occurs, we miss at least 50 percent of the learning opportunity.

For instance, we look at the forest fires in Yellowstone and think, "What a tragedy!" We look at the flooding of the Grand Canyon and say, "What a loss!" What we often fail to understand is that these are the necessary components of natural laws that bring life and regeneration by natural means. There are also natural laws that apply to the development and treatment of chemical imbalances that, when understood and managed, bring life and regeneration.

When we deal with depression or anxiety disorders, we tend to be overwhelmed by the apparent negativity of the symptoms. We are even more prone to believe that we are our symptoms. But we're not. In reality, we're so much more!

Symptoms are physical or emotional messages that we don't clearly understand. If we ignore these messages, they won't go away. If ignored, they tend to generate additional symptoms and discomfort. However, once we understand the messages, we should be able to control the symptoms. Unfortunately, because we so often misunderstand and misinterpret our symptoms, we do not see things as they really are. We see things as we are. And because of this distortion, we may believe that the way things appear to be is the way things will always be. But it's only an illusion.

The symptoms of chemical imbalances are like intransigent teachers—they push us, they punish us, but invariably they lead us to levels of emotional and spiritual depth that were previously unattainable. Where once only chaos, incorrect principles, and painful life experiences existed, these symptoms—when redefined and reformed—allow for coalescence and integration of mind, body, and spirit. These are the gifts of chemical imbalances.

If we fail to understand the role these gifts play in life, then we will ultimately fail to learn what only they can teach us. But if we recognize them for what they really are—teachers—the things we discover and learn to understand will stretch our minds. And once stretched, they will never return to their original dimensions.

TREATMENT: IT MAY NOT BE WHAT YOU EXPECT

Depression and anxiety disorders may well be described as a war zone. And like the movement of armed forces committed to the destruction of its enemy, the unrelenting cadence marches from confusion, to impairment, to paralysis. The result is often an escalating loss of control that may seem to be overwhelming and all consuming. Without the ability to redefine these problems in a manner that makes them manageable, it would be easy to believe their discouraging message of futility. But don't believe it!

We must remember that there is a time and a season for all things and that there is purpose in both the positive and the painful. These problems are teachers, and as such, we are meant to accept, understand, and integrate them—not merely endure them. In this manner, they encourage each of us to rise above them, to grow because of them, and to learn what only they can teach.

Success in this endeavor consists not merely of passing through life but of allowing life to pass through us. As this process takes place, it becomes possible to separate and incorporate those principles that we've been prepared to accept, while letting the other principles filter through us as seeds that will undoubtedly germinate at some time in the future. This is what treatment is all about. It's a process, not of termination and finality but of appreciation, anticipation, and management. That is, appreciation for the emotional depth and personal insight that has resulted from the painful experiences, anticipation that the best is yet to come, and management of the conflicts rather than control or domination.

Because of the intensity of overcoming our previous selves, we must remember that total success does not mean giving up our imperfections totally but rather improving a little at a time. This is where treatment begins. This is where life begins.

NOTES

1.   *The American Heritage Dictionary*, 2nd ed., s.v. "Will" (Boston: Houghton Mifflin, 1982).

CHAPTER 2

A CHILD OF GOD

AS A YOUNG CHILD, I HAD NO IDEA OUR HOME LIFE WAS different from others. As a teenager, it became evident that something was wrong. However, it wasn't until my adult years that I realized we were victims of abuse. We were powerless as children to prevent what happened in our home. Although it has taken almost forty years to overcome the effects—about the same length of time it took the children of Israel to find their way out of the wilderness—I can now look back and say that it contributed to my spiritual development. I'm stronger today because I learned to put my trust in God.

Over the years, especially as a teenager, I found it extremely difficult to attend church and listen to sermons about love at home and how home can be like heaven on earth. It was even more challenging when they spoke about enjoying loving relationships with their parents. I became somewhat cynical whenever we were encouraged to be united as a family and to spend more time together. I generally had three reactions. My initial reaction was one of disbelief. I thought they must have been exaggerating when they spoke about the loving interactions they had with their parents. My second reaction was usually a feeling of sadness as I wondered what I was doing wrong since my experiences at home didn't match what I was hearing. My third reaction was a feeling of bitterness and disillusionment as I yearned to have the same experiences others seemed to enjoy.

I didn't realize the ideal of a loving, harmonious family is just that—an ideal. God and our religious leaders have given us a standard to strive for. Some of us are closer to that standard than others. Nevertheless, having a perfect family is not a prerequisite for experiencing God's love.

As hard as it was for me to listen to, understand, and even learn from stories of healthy family experiences, I recognized the need for religion to teach and focus on healthy families. I learned that I needed to focus on achieving this goal rather than on comparing my situation to the ideal. I also needed to seek out the support necessary to build the type of family I yearned for.

It has taken a long time, but I no longer react as I once did to stories about happy families. I still feel a sense of loss because I don't have the healthy, loving relationship with my parents that I long for. I love them because they are my parents, and, with the help of the infinite atonement, I have forgiven them. However, I have a different definition of forgiveness now, that is, letting go of false hope for a better past and giving up the self-destructive anger and cynicism that accompanies continually dashed hopes.

The teachings of Christ have given me a pattern and a way of life to follow. However, I discovered that despite my best efforts and resolution to improve upon my heritage, I was unable to change my parents. I could only apply these principles to my own emotional and spiritual journey.

For example, during the first twenty years of our marriage my wife, Laurie, and I assumed what was perceived to be our responsibility for extended family members. As the oldest son, I mistakenly believed I was responsible for my parents' feelings, choices, and well-being. I usually found myself in the middle of their personal problems and ultimately felt intense anxiety and guilt when unable to fix them. I would frequently wonder why my parents didn't do the same things for me. Why were they oblivious to my needs? Why was I so unappreciated? The counsel I gave them was unwanted and unused. As a result, I often felt hurt. This led to feelings of frustration, anger, disappointment, and resentment.

Despite attempts to intervene after I left home, abuse of my younger siblings persisted. Four of my younger siblings were eventually removed from home and placed in foster care. A state social worker asked us to care for my youngest brother, who was only twelve years old at the time. He suffered from severe emotional problems. We did the best we could to manage his frequent emotional outbursts and attempts to hurt himself. A few years later, he was placed in the state hospital. Another brother who had experienced extensive physical abuse lived with us for a year as we attempted to address his drug and alcohol problems. We worked with school personnel to try to keep him in high school; however, he eventually dropped out, which increased our sense of frustration and feelings of helplessness.

Numerous times, especially late at night, my father would call and demand that I help resolve arguments between him and my mother. On two separate occasions, because of his out-of-control behavior, I had no choice but to take him to the hospital and have him admitted to the psychiatric ward until he was stable enough to return home. This was one of the hardest things I've ever had to do in my life. I hated myself for having to do it, but I recognized that my mother and younger brothers and sisters needed someone to protect them from further harm.

When my younger siblings were no longer living at home, things calmed down, and I improved at establishing healthy boundaries. But a serious situation developed that caused my mother to be concerned for her safety. Laurie and I tried to help. At the end of several weeks, the only result of our efforts was that my father told us to stay out of their family matters—to leave and never come back!

This was a significant turning point for us. My father was right. We had no business being involved with their family problems, nor did we have the power to change them. We continued to pray for them, but we decided not get caught up in their personal issues, even when they attempted to drag us back into their dysfunction.

In the fall of 2007, I went back to visit with my parents after an absence of six years. I wanted to resolve in my mind that I had forgiven them for years of manipulation and abuse. During the visit, my mother told me she couldn't understand why I had not come sooner because they had forgiven us. Shocked by her comment, I had to ask myself, "Forgiven us for what?" We were pulled into situations nobody else in the family wanted to address, and now we needed their forgiveness?

The past several years have been life changing because I couldn't truly heal and forgive them until I was kicked out of the family. I now have a better perspective of things as they really are. However, pulling away from such family dynamics and escaping the feelings of guilt and distress that accompany separation initially requires great effort. The process is much like grieving the death of a loved one.

Years ago, when I was asked to participate in a family counseling session to help my youngest sister address the issues she was experiencing with our father, the counselor told us that our father was incapable of love and we shouldn't expect it from him. He was right. My father struggled to love God, himself, and all others in his life. Despite how painful it was to accept, and how much I longed for his love, I concluded that a healthy relationship wasn't possible.

Over the years, I've struggled to understand what it means to honor my parents. I now know the best way we can honor our parents is to live the teachings of Jesus Christ. We also honor them by not enabling abuse. There comes a time in everyone's life when the best thing that can be done for others is to let them exercise their agency and reap the consequences of their choices, rather than continue to make excuses for their behavior and attempt to bail them out of situations they should be figuring out for themselves. One of the greatest challenges of being in an unhealthy relationship is recognizing whether our actions are helpful or whether they are enabling or exacerbating the situation.

After many years of working to overcome the effects of my past, I can now say those early experiences ultimately helped increase my faith in God. Unfortunately, I cannot say this is the case for many of my siblings. I've learned that at some point in our lives, we must each accept responsibility for our attitudes and actions and make a conscious choice to move forward and not continue in destructive patterns of behavior that simply do not help us to fulfill our real purpose in life. We must press forward and seek out the support we need to heal. It serves no purpose to continue blaming our parents, environment, or biological predispositions for the choices we make.

I now know that forgiveness does not mean we continue engaging in the same thinking and behavioral patterns. We have to change! I have forgiven my parents, but I have a greater responsibility to my immediate family and to myself in order to break the generational chains of dysfunction. Growing up, I learned several incorrect principles in my home, such as emotional dependency, poor self-image, impaired coping techniques, fear, and various other types of faulty-thinking patterns that influence all areas of life.

Healing emotionally has taken a long time. As an adult, I'm now striving to remember that I am a child of God. Not one filled with fear, but one to whom God has given joy, happiness, wonder, the ability to live in the present, and an appreciation of repetition and of the beauty that is all around us. Recognizing we are children of a loving God requires perseverance. It's a process of discovery during which we learn that God loves us even though we may still be struggling to love ourselves.

CLINICAL INSIGHTS

REMEMBER WHO YOU ARE

Carolyn S. Brown once related the following story in a speech: A little boy was watching Michelangelo as he sculpted the statue of David. But as the artist removed one small chip at a time, the young boy became restless. Because of his limited perception, all he could see was a shapeless mass of granite, and, after a short time, he lost interest and left. Months later, he returned just as Michelangelo was finishing the work of art. Looking at the statue, he asked almost reverently, "How did you know he was in there?"[1]

And so it is with each of us. Rarely are we able to see ourselves accurately. We often focus on our supposedly shapeless masses or on the pain that results as the chips are chiseled away by our losses and difficult life experiences. In reality, these chips are key components in the refining process. And as they are removed, we eventually discover the work of art inside. Ironically, from what appears to be a painful process of loss, we develop the gifts of insight, understanding, and wisdom.

We're all in some stage of being prepared to make a difference. The problems we encounter and the successes and failures we experience are all part of the discovery and developmental processes that ultimately define our lives. As this process unfolds, we're drawn into the lives of others in order to touch, teach, motivate, and love them.

Because of our limited perception, things tend to get complicated, and we get off track as we engage in a variety of self-defeating behaviors. In essence, we get ourselves into a hole and keep ourselves there by denying, rationalizing, or justifying our position. When this happens, we need to remember "The First Rule of Holes": when you're in one, stop digging!

Life can be confusing, and our performance is often misjudged to be equal to our worth. But performance does not equal worth. Worth exists even when it hasn't been discovered. To clarify this distinction, we are not what happened in the past with its pain, mistakes, and devastation. We are not what is happening now, with all of our symptoms, addictions, and self-defeating behaviors. And we are not what will happen in the future with all our fears, anxieties, and uncertainties. While each of these dynamic forces contributes to the discovery and development of who we really are, the most significant factor is what we become as a result of them. In reality, we are so much more than any of them.

In the movie *The Lion King*, the young lion Simba has a similar experience. He is running from himself and from his past. In a dramatic scene, his deceased father materializes in the clouds and says, "You have forgotten me. You have forgotten who you are, and so, you have forgotten me. Look inside yourself. You are more than you have become. Remember who you are."[2] How often are we like this? With all the problems and confusion in life, we tend to get lost. We avoid looking inside because we're so afraid we'll find nothing of value. So we run. We settle for less than who we really are.

Because of this, my guess is that if God were to come to us, he would say, "You have forgotten me. You have forgotten who you are, and so you have forgotten me. Look inside yourself. You are more than you have become. Remember who you are."

Regardless of our genetics, our training, or our experience, life is ultimately a choice. We can either choose to live life with purpose and get what we want, or we can choose to live life by accident and settle for whatever comes our way. It's always a choice. There really is a plan and a purpose to life, so don't settle for less. Always remember who you are.

HOW TO REMEMBER

Create a picture of yourself as you would like to be in the future and then practice being the kind of person you envision. You will become what you practice. Remember who you are.

Because of your experiences in life, you undoubtedly have developed a variety of intuitive skills that will enable you to understand others more effectively. All experiences can be converted into something beneficial. Value those characteristics. Remember who you are.

You will be able to contribute to the lives of those around you. It's not necessary that you know specifically what that contribution will be or when you will make it. Your significance will surface eventually. Remember who you are.

Make the decision to get along with difficult people. Don't let them control your happiness or sadness. Remember who you are.

Decide to look at conflict differently. Since it appears that there will always be conflict in life, the goal is to manage it in the most efficient way. Don't run from it or let it control you. Remember who you are.

Develop a sincere interest in others. Many people are so caught up with their own fears and concerns that they are almost incapable of seeing anything else. Everyone is fighting a battle. Let them know you understand. Remember who you are.

Look for the positive characteristics in others. Everyone has a combination of weak and strong personality traits. Whatever you look for, you'll find. Remember who you are.

Forgive the hurtful actions of others. Forgive everyone, even if they are unaware that you have done so. When you forgive others, you don't let them off the hook—you let yourself off the hook. Remember who you are.

Help others feel encouraged. Everyone needs to have his or her batteries recharged periodically. Because of the pains and disappointments you have experienced, you understand that need and can offer encouragement to others. Remember who you are.

Commit yourself to accept people as they are. There are reasons why people are the way they are, and you may never completely understand those reasons. You are an instrument to reach others. Remember who you are.

Be open to new relationships but remember that your worth is not dependent upon whether others approve of you or appreciate you. Accept the fact that there will always be those who are not ready for a relationship. Don't take it personally. Remember who you are.

WE MIGHT AS WELL DANCE

Each of us has been endowed with a portion of the good, the bad, and the ugly. Eventually, as these characteristics become converted into traits that guide and direct our lives, we are bound to some degree by these characteristics. As we grow and develop, the power and intensity of these patterns often increase to the point that they may seem to be almost impossible to eliminate. We're not alone. One way or another, everyone is fighting this battle!

Henry David Thoreau once wrote: "If one advances confidently in the direction of his dreams, to live the life which he has imagined, he will meet with success unexpected in common hours."[3] In other words, our happiness is simply a matter of perception, persistence, and perseverance.

Rising above the patterns of the past is often just a matter of subtleties. It's living, not just being alive. Life is meant to be more than mere existence—it was meant to be understood and managed and mastered. Life is choosing, not just having choices. We are meant to make choices and be stretched by the choices we make. Life is action, not just reaction. Life isn't meant to be controlled by the reactions of others but by the development of insight that comes from learning, succeeding, and failing. Life is creation, not just tolerance. Like the clay of the sculptor, life is meant to be molded into something of significance. In essence, as Frank Tyger wrote, "Your future depends on many things, but mostly you."[4]

The wise don't expect to find life worth living—they make it that way! What they do and what they become is merely a reflection of who they think they are. Edmund Burke wrote, "All that is necessary for the triumph of evil is that good men do nothing."[5] When we do nothing to take charge of life, our success has more to do with who we think we are than with any other single factor.

We need to redefine ourselves not by our worst days, but by our best. Not by the mistakes of the past, but by the principles we integrate in the present. Not by the circumstances of our birth and life, but by the attitudes we create. Not by what we say we're going to do, but by the choices we make and the behaviors we use.

Author and motivational speaker Marianne Williamson once wrote,

> Our deepest fear is not that we are inadequate. Our deepest fear is that we are powerful beyond measure. It is our light, not our darkness, that most frightens us. We ask ourselves, Who am I to be brilliant, gorgeous, talented, fabulous? Actually, who are you not to be? You are a child of God. Your playing small does not serve the world. There is nothing enlightened about shrinking so that other people won't feel insecure around you. We are all meant to shine, as children do. We were born to make manifest the glory of God that is within us. It's not just in some of us; it's in everyone. And as we let our own light shine, we unconsciously give other people permission to do the same. As we are liberated from our own fear, our presence automatically liberates others.[6]

Unfortunately, we often hesitate to take charge of our lives because of fear. We resist making the necessary changes until the pain is too great to continue and until we finally reach the point where we have nothing left to lose. At that point, the benefits of moving on are greater than the comforts of holding on, and we begin to change our course in life—in spite of the pain, not because of it. The initiation of this process is not an indication of failure, but an essential step that leads to success. With these principles of self-definition as a foundation, we can face our tests in life, and we can discover answers and develop insights that will determine our destinies. No, life may not be the party we hoped for, but—through our choices—we determine the music that accompanies us, and we might as well dance to it.

NOTES

1.   Carolyn S. Brown, "College: More than Papers, Tests, and Grades," devotional address at LDS Business College (Salt Lake City, Utah, January 22, 2008). http://www.ldsbc.edu/index.php?option=com_content&view=art icle&id=282:college-more-than-papers-tests-and-grades&catid=9:devotionals &Itemid=554 (accessed Dec. 12, 2011).

2.   "He Lives in You," *The Lion King*, Special Edition DVD, directed by Roger Allers and Rob Minkoff (Burbank, CA: Walt Disney Studios, 1994)."

3.   Henry David Thoreau, "Endeavors Quotes," accessed December 12, 2011, http://www.brainyquote.com/quotes/keywords/endeavors.html.

4.   Frank Tyger, "Frank Tyger Art Quotes," accessed December 12, 2011, http://www.quote.robertgenn.com/auth_search.php?authid=317.

5.   Edmund Burke, The Henrik Hudson School Disrict Libray Media Centre, accessed December 12, 2011, http://tartarus.org/~martin/essays/burkequote.html.

6.   SKDesigns, "Internet Resources," accessed January 2, 2012, http://skdesigns.com/internet/articles/quotes/williamson/our_deepest_fear. From Marianne Williamson, *A Return To Love: Reflections on the Principles of A Course in Miracles* (Harper Collins, 1992), 190–91.

CHAPTER 3

NEVER GIVE IN OR GIVE UP

ON OCTOBER 29, 1941, WINSTON CHURCHILL, THE BRITISH prime minister, spoke to the students at Harrow School in London. It was during World War II—a dark, fearful time for millions of people in England. He said, "Never give in, never, never . . . in nothing, great or small, large or petty—never give in except to convictions of honour and good sense. Never yield to force; never yield to the apparently overwhelming might of the enemy."[1]

Despite the overwhelming power of the German forces, the British didn't give in or give up, even when they were standing alone. They endured and, with the subsequent help of their allies, were able to turn what appeared to be inevitable destruction into ultimate victory. They were also willing to reach out for and accept support from their allies. A terrible, destructive force that had laid waste to all in its path was defeated by the determination and faith of a people who, under great burden and with great sorrow, continued to fight back. Their indomitable spirit was born in the depths of despair.

We see examples of perseverance in our day as well. They may not take place on battlefields or during times of war but rather in the silent battles we fight each day in our homes, schools, and communities. These battles are fought by individuals who want to have better lives and the courage to improve themselves, reach out for help, and seek after worthy goals.

Athletics is one area in which we see examples of perseverance and courage. For example, Chris Yergensen played football for the University of Utah. With Washington State University leading 31 to 28, Chris was called in to attempt a twenty-yard field goal in order to tie the game. Chris ran onto the field and got into position. The ball was snapped and placed upright, and then he kicked it. It went wide to the left. The Utes lost the hard-fought 1992 Copper Bowl game.

The coaches and fans were devastated, but none took it harder than Chris. He was so upset by the loss that he avoided his coaches and team members for days. A week later, his coach invited him into his office. He gave Chris two options—he could begin preparing for next year's football season, or he could quit.

Chris resolved to do all he could to prepare for the next season. With the help of supportive coaches, he devoted many hours to refining his skills. The following year in 1993, he redeemed himself when the Utes played against their biggest in-state rival: Brigham Young University (BYU). Utah had not beaten BYU for many years, and Chris helped make it happen. In the final seconds of the game, he kicked a fifty-five-yard field goal, resulting in the first Ute win over BYU in Provo since 1971.[2] Chris Yergensen persevered when the option for quitting was offered him, and he sought the help he needed to improve. That is what makes his story so great!

The will to keep trying and the desire to continue doing our very best, regardless of the difficulties we encounter, can make life meaningful. It's the process of persevering, notwithstanding our personal weaknesses, that enables us to enjoy the small victories along the way. Part of persevering involves seeking the support of others.

We all face challenges that, at times, appear to be insurmountable. It may be abuse, a disability, an addiction, mental illness, or a combination of these conditions that challenges us. One of my greatest challenges has been working to overcome the effects of abuse, which also included severe anxiety and depression.

My parents struggled to raise a family of eleven children on an educator's salary. They rarely agreed on how to resolve family problems and spent much of their time fighting. My memories of such conflict extend back to my earliest years as a toddler and continued until I was able to leave home at age eighteen. My father suffered from bipolar disorder, and my mother suffered the consequences of his illness. She was sick throughout most of our childhood. It seemed that my father was either angry and depressed or overzealous about one thing or another. His father was an alcoholic and had died at an early age from the effects of his addiction.

Physical and emotional abuse was a regular part of our family life. We didn't recognize it as abuse back then; rather, we accepted it as a routine part of our daily existence. As children, we naively assumed this was how most fathers behaved. It wasn't until our adult years that we recognized it for what it was—abuse. We learned at an early age that our personal welfare was directly related to our willingness to pretend to submit to our father's will, which varied daily depending upon his mood.

I commonly felt sadness, low self-esteem, anxiety, and fear during adolescence, and these feelings carried over to adulthood. I don't doubt they had biological as well as environmental origins. Nevertheless, that was the package I was given. Two generations had now suffered from abuse. I needed to break the generational chain of dysfunction for my future family. It was up to me to make the most of the situation by working with these personal challenges, seeking out support, and striving to find the happiness and joy that seemed to elude me as a child.

Fortunately in our community there were excellent youth sports programs. Sports were my outlet. I was blessed with athletic ability and excelled in basketball, baseball, and football. When playing sports, I forgot about the challenges at home. I enjoyed the praise of teammates, coaches, and spectators. Their praise helped me to feel good about myself. When playing sports, I felt like a whole person. Yet I could not extend that feeling of wholeness to other aspects of my life.

During adolescence, I struggled with severe anxiety and feelings of worthlessness and became more withdrawn at school. I was a good student but had so little confidence that I was terrified when asked to read aloud. I avoided any opportunity to speak in front of others and tried hard to remain invisible during class time. Isolation wasn't the answer, and my depression increased during this time. However, the desire to participate in sports, combined with fervent prayer, helped me to survive those turbulent years.

In high school I reached a point where my depression was so intense that I felt I didn't have the emotional strength to continue playing on the school basketball team. I had already quit playing baseball and football due to anxiety and depression. Basketball was my greatest love, and now I was considering quitting the team.

I remember walking into the locker room my junior year to visit with the basketball coach. I told him I couldn't continue playing. He spoke with me for a while and said he would not let me quit. He asked me to do the best I could for the rest of the season. I hung in and somehow made it through, thanks in part to his support.

The next year, as a senior, I again played on the school team. I continued to struggle with anxiety and depression. Nevertheless, our team enjoyed a successful season and won the region championship. At the end of the season, three trophies were awarded to members of the varsity basketball team—one to the top scorer, one to the top rebounder, and one to the outstanding defensive player—me. The coach said the award was for the player who gave 110% on the court. That meant a lot to me, especially since I would have quit playing the year before without his support. The award represented my ability not only to persevere a little longer but also to do my best despite intense personal challenges at home. Thanks to this caring coach, I was beginning to learn that doing your best, regardless of your insecurities, does matter. I learned that when you choose to keep trying and accept support as it's offered, you create opportunities for further success.

Several years after graduating from high school, I married my high school sweetheart, Laurie. She has been—and continues to be—a wonderful wife and mother. The best decision I ever made was to ask her to marry me. She is my best friend. Our love for each other has matured significantly since those early years. My life has become so much more complete and meaningful since marrying her. Laurie recognizes my potential and has worked to assist me in realizing it. I strive to do the same for her. I love her with all my heart and look forward each evening to coming home from work to be with her.

During the early part of our marriage, I continued to struggle to overcome the effects of my past. Regardless of what I attempted to do, it seemed that I heard my father's voice in my head telling me I couldn't do it. This was especially true with regard to pursuing a college education. I had to learn to replace the loud voice of the past with the still, small voice of the present, which prompted me to keep trying a little longer.

My father seemed to project his own inadequacies and weaknesses onto his children. If he couldn't do something, he provided little encouragement for us to attempt it. For example, he discouraged me from pursuing a doctoral degree because of the difficulties associated with completing the statistics courses and writing a dissertation.

Shortly after marrying Laurie, I obtained a teaching certificate, taught high school, and began attending graduate school. I eventually reached the point in graduate school where all the coursework was successfully completed and it was time to begin writing my doctoral dissertation. With all of the data gathered and preliminary work completed, all that was left to do was write.

This was another defining moment in my life. Still struggling with the effects of depression, facing the challenges of trying to be a good husband and father and working full-time, I was overwhelmed. I was ready to give up on the dissertation and my dream of earning a PhD. It's not uncommon for students to complete their graduate school coursework and never obtain their doctoral degrees because of the challenges associated with completing a dissertation. It's a demanding, time-consuming process. However, once again I was given encouraging counsel and support, this time from my wife, to continue to do my best. With her support and our fervent prayers, I was able to continue and finish the dissertation.

Over the years, I've come to understand that much of the happiness I enjoy today is built upon the personal triumphs of my past. These small victories were not achieved alone but were the direct result of help from supportive teachers, coaches, a loving wife, and a God who heard and answered my prayers by directing me to obtain the help I needed. My faith in God has been a tremendous source of strength throughout my life. I also now recognize the important role of appropriate counseling support and medical treatment in coping with mental health issues and the effects of abuse.

Our happiness and joy increase as we continue striving, with the support of others, to do our very best. We each face opposition, which at times may overwhelm us. We need not struggle alone. God blesses us through the spiritual gifts and talents of others. Such loving support from others can assist us in our efforts to endure the personal challenges we face. He also blesses us with unique strengths that can help us to persevere and grow from our afflictions rather than be destroyed by them. As we humbly seek God's guidance through sincere prayer, our trials and afflictions can serve to soften—not harden—our hearts.

CLINICAL INSIGHTS

STUMBLING BLOCKS OR STEPPING-STONES?

When life doesn't go the way we want it to, we often respond with questions like, "Why me? Why now? Why do I have to go through this?" But if we had greater insight, we would probably be more likely to ask, "What am I supposed to learn from this? What am I being prepared for? How will the future be different as a result of what I'm experiencing right now?" And "How will I be able to use this experience to make a positive difference in the world?"

Our lives are guided and coordinated in a manner that is sometimes difficult for us to comprehend. But simply because we don't fully understand this process, it does not negate the fact that there really is purpose, reason, and wisdom in life. Depression also has a purpose.

Depression seems to be the result of a complex interaction between certain genetic tendencies or predispositions combined with the thinking patterns we develop as we experience a variety of painful life events and poor life choices. However, things are not always the way that they appear. Life is miraculously filled with a wide variety of situations whose only purpose is to create our destiny. The thinking patterns or habits of explanation that we develop from dealing with these situations tend to help each of us develop a perception of helplessness or hopefulness, pessimism or optimism.

It's not simply a painful sequence of events that causes depression; rather, it's our perception of those events. Perception determines the ease or difficulty with which we make life-management decisions. Perception creates our reality.

While life generally inflicts similar levels of pain and problems on just about everyone, optimists tend to see these obstacles as stepping-stones that strengthen them and enable them to rise to a higher level of progression. The pain is still there, but optimists view it as something that can be managed. Pessimists tend to see the obstacles as stumbling blocks, which invariably lead to depression, anxiety, and frustration.

As a result, pessimists become controlled by the stumbling blocks. They tend to get depressed more easily, stay depressed longer, and relapse more easily after treatment. If something as simple as optimism can make you happier and healthier, make the choice to have it!

Look for the positive. Expect to find it. Learn from it. Manage it. Because when all is said and done, depression is never wasted. The optimist recognizes that things will get better. The hardships and challenges in life will not last forever but are a necessary part of the growth process. Optimists understand the principles identified below:

- Pain is the motivator, not the problem. You're going to experience pain as you go through life. Some people will get more of it than others, but everyone will get their share. That's important to understand because pain causes change and change causes growth. There's no other way.

- You have a purpose, and there is a plan. Believe it or not, there are some things in this life that only you can do. You have a purpose. There is a plan for your being. It just takes a while to figure out what it is.

- Problems are the answers to prayers. As you meet the various challenges in life, you will discover the special characteristics with which you have been endowed.

- When the student is ready, the teacher will appear. No matter what happens to you, you will never be completely alone. A number of people will be brought into your life to help you manage it and find your way home.

- Lessons will continue. Your life will be full of lessons, and God's plan permits you to learn at your own speed. If you're not ready to understand the lesson, it will be repeated until you are.

- Nothing is wasted. No matter what happens, and no matter how big a mistake you make, learn from it, put it behind you, and move on. Most of the greatest learning comes from our mistakes. Remember, failing is not failure!

- Develop an attitude of gratitude. Since your attitude will determine your happiness, look for the beauty in life and expect only the best. More often than not, you'll find it.

- Never accept mediocrity. You can't afford not to try your best.

- You are not your symptoms. Symptoms are simple, misunderstood messages that are trying to tell us something. Once you understand the messages, the symptoms will become manageable.

- Finally, and most important, never give in or give up—never, never! There are many solutions to every problem in life. One of them will work!

EVENTUALLY

Eventually, if we don't give up and we keep doing what needs to be done, things will begin to settle down in life, both inside and outside of us. We finally realize that life is not an endurance contest or a competition with fate, but rather a process of discovery. As we wrestle with our thoughts, feelings, and secrets during this transitional phase, a picture of who we are materializes.

Everything we do and everything that is done to us somehow becomes transformed onto the canvas of our lives. As this miraculous transformation takes place, our senses expand and merge into a kaleidoscope of intuition and awareness, resulting in influences that alter our personalities. Somewhere in the process, we begin to notice that we're more balanced, more complete, and more alive to the influences in and around us.

We also discover an inner voice—a guiding influence that leads us to greater personal acceptance and less inner conflict. The world itself doesn't change, but our hearts do, which causes us to view the world differently. In essence, the calm before the storm expands until it is able to overcome the storm altogether.

We become more aware of the current in life that is life-giving and life-enhancing, and we become more able to focus on the significance of the journey and less on confusion and fear. With this awareness, we develop a greater capacity to understand and accept that the responsibility for this process lies directly on our shoulders. In life, we can either make excuses or recognize results, and making excuses won't get us anywhere.

With this new awakening, we realize that if we really believe in the beauty of eternity, then we must learn to appreciate the splendor of each day. Without this appreciation, we participate in life, but we have no real freedom. Ultimate freedom depends on freedom to choose, freedom to choose our own path, and freedom to have no regrets for the paths we didn't choose.

As we choose to let go of our regrets, even though the pain and problems don't disappear completely, everything—even the past—tends to fall into place. We accept that we weren't perfect and that we made mistakes, but that was then, and this is now. Then we move on.

We finally get a glimpse of eternity as we realize that we're part of something much greater than ourselves. As we take part in this never-ending state of change, we begin to understand that everything is as it should be.

LIFE: SOME ASSEMBLY REQUIRED

Don't worry. Things are not as bad as they seem. They couldn't be! I'll admit that there are times things look a little bleak, but those times pass. They always pass.

I think that reality sums life up pretty well. It's a journey, an experience, and a process of discovery. It's an opportunity to examine correct and incorrect principles and then to decide which ones fit—like an emotional juggling act that allows us to clearly define our personalities. In the process, we eventually discover that we're headstrong and controlling as well as tender and caring.

We talk of losing ourselves in the service of our fellow men, but we usually do what we think is in our best interest. We admire humility and meekness, but we are often self-centered. We profess honesty and integrity, but we clearly rationalize and minimize our actions in our own favor.

We are known by many, loved by some, and despised by a few, and we consistently return those feelings, each for each. Even worse, we allow the reactions of others to determine how we feel about ourselves.

As further evidence of our insecurities, we constantly compare ourselves to others and measure our achievements by what others have done. So what's the solution to this dilemma?

Experience!

Experience is the name we give to our mistakes. It's how we pay our dues. Through experience, we eventually learn that it's not enough to be good—we have to be good for something. That means we must have commitment, dedication, and direction.

Achievement doesn't just happen by itself. It's always the result of natural laws. Two of the most important natural laws are growth and decay. Simply put, when we stop growing and developing, we begin to decay and die. This puts the responsibility for our success in our own hands. As the popular saying goes, "We have two ends with a common link. With one we sit, with one we think. Success depends on which you use. Heads, you win. Tails, you lose."

This means you can't sit on your bottom and slide to the top. It requires a lot of effort to be successful and even more to be happy. And there's a difference. Success simply means getting what you want. Happiness means wanting what you get.

It sounds confusing, but fortunately the instructions for both are relatively simple. They can be summed up in four words—life: some assembly required.

NOTES

1. Winston Churchill, The Churchill Centre, accessed December 12, 2011, http://www.winstonchurchill.org/learn/speeches/quotations.

2. JoAnn Jacobsen-Wells with Ron McBride, *Mac Attack!* (Riverton, Utah: Slickrock Books, 1998), 129–30.

CHAPTER 4

THE POWER OF PRAYER

I'M GRATEFUL FOR THE POWER OF PRAYER IN OUR LIVES. It's a tremendous blessing to know that we can approach God in humble prayer and seek his direction. I've learned a great deal about sincere prayer and faith in God by listening to the personal prayers of our children. Over the years, my wife, Laurie, has recorded in her journal some of the things our children would say. With our youngest son's permission, I'll share what he said when he was a child:

> Heavenly Father, help me when I find myself in a bad situation to think, what would Jesus do?
>
> Help me to do well in my soccer game tomorrow and help our team to win, but help us to remember that playing soccer is fun whether we win or lose.

My earliest experience with earnest, heartfelt prayer was at age fifteen. It seemed that there was constant turmoil and contention in our home. My parents were usually upset at each other for one reason or another. On one occasion, after a particularly long fight between them, I remember quietly retreating to the backyard, looking up at the stars, and wondering if things would ever improve.

I desperately wanted us to be a happy family, to have the peace and love in our home that we had been taught about in church. Before I knew it, I was kneeling down on the grass and pleading with God for help. I pled with all my heart that we could have love in our home. I knew that if such a thing were possible, God would be able to grant it. I prayed longer that evening than I had ever prayed before, and afterward received a calm reassurance that all would be well.

Unfortunately, things didn't change much in our home. However, throughout my teenage years, I didn't give up hope and continued to pray for my parents and for our family. Eventually, I married and had my own family. Several years after we had our third child, we gathered together and had a discussion about prayer. As we were discussing how God answers our prayers in his own way and time, I suddenly had a powerful confirmation inside that the heartfelt prayer offered years before had been answered. I was now blessed with a home where we enjoyed the love and peace that I had yearned for as a youth. How grateful I am to God for this blessing.

God hears our sincere prayers and answers them in the way he knows is best for each of us. In our struggle to escape the pain, it's easy to forget that his timetable for answering and ours for receiving answers are not always the same. One of the challenges of overcoming the effects of abuse and other unhealthy patterns of behavior is learning to focus on our blessings instead of on our burdens. This does not mean we need to deny the pain; rather, we need to be careful not to become consumed by it, thereby making it more difficult to recognize answers to our prayers.

Throughout most of my life I've struggled to forgive my father. I carried the burden of unforgiveness for many years, while he remained unaware of wrongdoing. Over the years, my wife would point out that I needed to move on, to forgive, and to let go of those thoughts and feelings. By holding on to such resentment, I added large stones to the spiritual wall I had built between God and me in the form of feelings of unworthiness, shame, and guilt. These additional stones made it more difficult to recognize answers to prayer and receive much-needed guidance.

I didn't know how to move on because those thoughts were so much a part of me. They were firmly embedded in the wall I had created. They made it difficult for me to recognize the many ways God had already blessed me. I've learned that such thoughts and feelings are thieves. They steal away our peace and our ability to live in the present. They make it difficult to receive or recognize answers to prayer.

Most of us have had similar experiences. Someone in our lives may have done something to us or said something that hurt our feelings. We can't let it go and allow resentful thoughts to fester. We may struggle to forgive that person.

I've discovered that as we work hard to let go of grudges and forgive others, we pull down one of the larger stones in the wall we may have built. The stone of unforgiveness must be removed if we are to heal emotionally and progress spiritually. It may require effort, humility, fervent prayer, and even professional counseling, but, once removed, we will be able to feel God's love more freely.

Not all prayers are answered immediately. Some answers may not come for a long time. Other times we may need to make certain changes in our lives, thoughts, and actions in order to recognize the answers. With the habit of sincere prayer firmly in place, miracles do happen. Humble, earnest prayer helps us change and align our will with God's. It helps us to more clearly see the light of the Lord through the thick darkness of shame, despair, and fear.

CLINICAL INSIGHTS

REFLECTIONS ON THE SERENITY PRAYER

Simple, direct, and effective, the anonymously authored Serenity Prayer is a good foundation for peace of mind and a more balanced perspective. When understood and personalized, it applies to everyone. Yet it means something different to each of us.

Serenity is not freedom from the storm, but peace amid the storm. It's the result of a change in perception that occurs in spite of ourselves. Without this state of mind, we tend to get high strung. When we're high strung, we're usually out of tune with reality.

Courage is the quality from which heroes are made. Heroes are all around us. They include those who endure when they want to quit, those who overcome challenges in the face of fear, and those who choose to grow in spite of their pain. Courage is doing what must be done. It's taking a stand for what's right, especially when there's pressure to do otherwise. Courage is backbone, not wishbone.

Wisdom—true wisdom—is not knowing all. It's knowing what to

do with what you know. It's being aware of your strengths and knowing the limitations of your knowledge. Wisdom may be recognized through the application of two very important principles: "Don't sweat the small stuff," and remember, "It's all small stuff."[1]

The combination of serenity, courage, and wisdom can bring about impressive changes in life. These attributes develop at different times in response to various crises or mistakes from which lessons were learned.

When the situations are right and we rise to a level where our perception becomes more accurate, the synergism that results from that combination adds a new dimension to life. Our vision becomes forever altered. So look to the future. The best is yet to come!

TRUSTING YOURSELF

In life we are either a light or a shadow, a guide who assists others in discovering the path or merely a part of the confusion and darkness. Becoming is a developmental process that often stops and starts and changes direction numerous times.

As a result of this process, we develop a variety of gifts that we take with us throughout life. While some people seem to have more of these gifts than others, it appears that the specific gifts we have enable us to touch the lives of those around us in a manner that is unique and incomparable.

Undoubtedly, these gifts are not just for our own use because they unify and strengthen everyone who is touched by them. Sometimes we hesitate to use them. Sometimes we simply don't trust ourselves to do so.

Life provides a wealth of experience, and experience is a power that guides and directs our destinies. Experience teaches that we have always managed to survive everything that has happened to us in the past, in one way or another, and it gives us confidence that we will be able to survive in the future. To do so requires that we must learn to trust ourselves. Unless we trust ourselves, it's virtually impossible to trust anyone else. Yet trusting yourself goes far beyond that simple concept.

Trusting yourself means first trusting in God and in his infinite power to bless you. It means prayerfully seeking his guidance and striving to do his will. Trusting yourself means accepting the present moment for what it is, even though you don't know for certain what may happen in the future.

Trusting yourself means allowing others to say what they may say, without feeling that you have to decipher all the hidden messages behind what they say.

Trusting yourself means accepting yourself for what you really are and having the confidence to believe that what you really are is what you will become. Your real worth is something that far exceeds even your wildest imagination.

Trusting yourself means accepting the fact that happiness is not an illusion nor is it elusive or beyond your reach. Happiness is a natural by-product of trusting yourself.

Trusting yourself means setting limits with yourself, setting boundaries with others, and setting realistic expectations both for yourself and others.

Trusting yourself means making mistakes, learning from them, and rising above them. Mistakes are not signs of inadequacy or failure but are a natural part of living and learning.

Trusting yourself is an essential preparatory step to managing the trials and tribulations in life. Without this trust there would be hesitancy, discouragement, and ultimately a lesser degree of happiness.

Trusting yourself means allowing yourself to be alone without fearing that you'll be lonely forever and allowing yourself to be involved with others without fearing that you'll lose yourself in the relationship.

Trusting yourself makes it possible to trust others, and that makes it possible to love them. In essence, trusting yourself means having the courage to outgrow your previous self.

Trusting yourself means not waiting for an invitation to participate in life. All too frequently, we allow the reactions of others to determine the choices we make. While this provides a type of comfort and predictability, it impairs our ability to take charge of life. Once this pattern becomes deeply embedded, it becomes difficult to break. That which becomes familiar becomes normal, even if normal is painful and limiting.

Trusting yourself means developing an attitude of gratitude. This makes it possible to appreciate both positive and painful experiences in life, to benefit from the lessons they teach, and to grow from the maturity and insight they leave behind. Specifically, it's not happiness that makes us grateful, but it's an attitude of gratitude that makes us happy.

Trusting yourself means recognizing that you are a part of everyone and everything. You're not separate. You're never alone. It is fear that makes you think you are alone.

Trusting yourself means accepting the fact that while life comes with uncertainty and anxiety, it also comes with the tools and techniques to manage those trials and rise above them.

Trusting yourself does not mean having a fortress that protects you from all unfortunate events but rather a stronghold that provides freedom and peace of mind to help you face problems and difficulties with confidence and equanimity.

Trusting yourself means allowing yourself to dream, to rise above your limitations, to visualize who you are becoming, and to take an active part in the creation of that person.

Trusting yourself means knowing the difference between the inner child and the adult. Both are significant parts of who you are. When you feel the inner child part of you (with all the feelings of helplessness and hopelessness), when old memories try to convince you that you're not big enough or strong enough, and when fear tries to overwhelm you and tell you that something terrible is about to happen, remember—you're a grown-up now.

Finally, continue to remind yourself that trusting yourself means forgiving yourself, forgiving those who failed to appreciate you in the past, and forgiving those who fail to recognize who you are now. Forgiving others doesn't let them off the hook. It allows you to move on with your life in spite of them. Trusting yourself means forgiveness, and forgiveness means freedom!

THE POWER OF PERCEPTION

Things are seldom as bad as they appear to be. We all know that. And yet, when we're feeling miserable, somehow we forget what we know as we slip back into the tried and tested perception of fear and insecurity. Feelings are the result of chemical reactions in our bodies, and when we have a chemical imbalance, our perception becomes a chemical figment of our imagination. When this occurs and everything seems chaotic, we have two choices: we can attempt to change our perception, or we can try to prove there is no need to do so.

Given these two options, we generally tend to avoid change at all costs, even when this avoidance means the pain will continue. Another interesting pattern of human nature is that the way we see others is often a reflection of how we see ourselves. In other words, when we're negative and critical of others, it may be an indication that we have similar views of ourselves.

When we have difficulty trusting others, we may have a history of not trusting ourselves. If we believe something long enough, it either is true or it becomes true. As a result, we push ourselves to the point that we don't know whom to trust. Hence, we systematically sabotage ourselves and separate ourselves from everyone because we feel that they just don't understand!

We are the only ones who can stop the insanity. It all starts with making new choices. If we keep on doing what we've done, we're going to keep on getting what we've been getting. Unfortunately, when we struggle too much with our problems in life, sometimes we miss out on the lessons they teach. The process of change starts with a change in perception. It's not easy. In fact, some would say it's impossible. In reality, while the "difficult" takes time, the "impossible" just takes a little longer.

The good news is that we don't have to go through this process of change alone. Once we make the commitment, the powers of providence move into action, preparing us for what's to come and bringing individuals into our lives who can assist us. With this in mind, there's an ancient prayer that emphasizes this principle: "God, help me to be thankful for assistance that's already on its way from unseen sources." Miracles do occur, and healing does take place. So keep your expectations high, because no one ever rises to low expectations.

NOTES

1.   Richard Carlson, *Don't Sweat the Small Stuff . . . and It's All Small Stuff* (New York: Hyperion, 1997).

CHAPTER 5

THE LIGHTHOUSE OF THE LORD

IN JOHN 8:12, JESUS TEACHES, "I AM THE LIGHT OF THE world; he that followeth me shall not walk in darkness, but shall have the light of life." The lighthouse of the Lord beckons all of us to follow.

Several years ago, my family and I spent a week on the beautiful Oregon coast. During our trip, we saw several lighthouses and were able to tour one known as Heceta Head. This lighthouse could emit a beam of light over twenty-five miles out to sea. It could emit its light through dense fog far enough to protect ships and boats from any potential hazards. We also discovered that each lighthouse emits a different pattern of intervals of light and darkness, which serves as a navigational point so that ships passing by at night or sailing in a thick fog can tell where they are in relation to the coastal region and can avoid any dangerous rocks or shoals.

The crews of ships sailing along the cost rely upon these lighthouses for direction and safety. They are even more dependent upon the lighthouses during stormy, turbulent, and foggy conditions. Without the light, sailors easily lose their way, crash their ships against the jagged rocks, and are destroyed.

At times, we find ourselves caught in the turbulent storms of life. These storms come in the form of loneliness, despair, depression and anxiety, fear, abuse, or disability. During these times, it is even more important that we strive to follow the light of the Lord. Although the light may seem distant and dim, we are blessed and comforted as we continue to follow it.

During my teenage years and into adulthood, I battled with anxiety and depression. Trying to provide my parents with ongoing emotional support seemed to exacerbate these conditions. I became obsessive as I worked to create conditions that were predictable and safe. I mistakenly believed that if I committed myself to doing everything right, then my parents would be happy, I would feel better, and God would love me.

It took a long time, but I finally learned that God loves us no matter what, and we don't have to earn his love. It's always there! And while the effects of abuse are painful, I discovered that many of our struggles are not designed to punish us but to offer us opportunities to spiritually grow and develop.

I slowly began to understand that God loves us because we are his children. His son, Jesus Christ, loves us so much that he willingly suffered for all of our sins, weaknesses, and abuses in order to fully understand and strengthen each of us.

Despite this knowledge, I continued to struggle with anxiety, depression, and obsessive thoughts for many years. Over the years, I prayed regularly and fervently for help in overcoming these challenges. I was striving to do everything right. I would have been healed if my efforts alone were sufficient. However, the emotional pain persisted.

For most of my life, I erroneously believed that taking medication for anxiety and depression was a sign of weakness. I believed that church attendance, prayer, service to others, and scripture study were all that was necessary to be healed. My wife would periodically suggest that if I had diabetes, I wouldn't hesitate to take insulin. Like any other medical condition, a mental health concern requires treatment. Acting on her counsel and encouragement, I reluctantly scheduled a medical evaluation with my physician. He prescribed medication that made a noticeable difference. I no longer struggled as seriously with the effects of anxiety and depression. However, my emotional healing wasn't complete.

At different times during our lives, we find ourselves asking, "How do I obtain relief from pain and sorrow?" We know that when Christ fulfilled his mortal mission, he was ridiculed, betrayed, spat upon, and eventually crucified by those he dearly loved and diligently served. He experienced great pain and suffering when his quivering flesh was nailed to the cross, but the greatest of all suffering occurred in Gethsemane where he experienced the agonies of the atonement.

I've learned that I could do all the right things and say all the right words, but my efforts alone were not enough. Until I submitted my will to God, I simply couldn't be healed emotionally and progress spiritually. I needed to learn to love God, accept his love for me, and take advantage of the support he made available through others. In order to reap the full benefits of the atonement, I needed to become spiritually submissive. I believe that seeking help from others is part of the process of becoming spiritually submissive.

This principle was powerfully illustrated during a recent white-water canoeing trip down the Snake River near Jackson Hole, Wyoming. I went with another adult and a group of seventeen- and eighteen-year-old young men. During the time of year that we went, the rapids were especially strong and the water ice cold. Prior to taking the trip, our river guide carefully instructed us about how to navigate the rapids. He said that when we pass through the fast moving rapids, it's best to kneel down low in the canoe and paddle hard until we're in calm water again. Thinking that I knew something about canoeing, I casually listened to his instruction, strapped on my life jacket, and then pushed the canoe out into the river along with my seventeen-year-old son, who sat in the front of our canoe. Not more than three minutes had passed during our trip down the Snake when we hit the fast-moving King Rapids. Our canoe began to be tossed back and forth. In response, I did exactly what the guide said not to do—grabbed hold of the sides in an attempt to steady the canoe. In seconds, the canoe, my son, and I were pulled under the rapids. When we emerged, breathless because of the icy-cold water, we clung tightly to the overturned canoe while gasping for air as we continued down the river. Fortunately, our skilled guide was able to assist us with getting back into the canoe.

Unfortunately, just a few minutes later, the same scenario repeated itself. We hit another set of rapids, I grabbed on to the sides of the canoe to steady it, and we were immediately pulled under by the fast-moving water and churning whirlpools. Our river guide once again came to our rescue. Exhausted, bruised, and shivering, I was now humbled by the experience and determined to follow the guide's counsel to kneel down and paddle hard when passing through the rapids. As a result, the rest of the ten-mile trip down the river was successful. I managed to keep the canoe upright.

As we humble ourselves and kneel and seek God's guidance through prayer, we need to recognize that he may not always remove our trials, but he will always help us find the strength to endure them as we continue to strive to do his will. This strength may also sometimes come through the rescuing support and service of others he sends into our lives in times of need.

In Matthew 11:28–30, we read: "Come unto me, all ye that labour and are heavy laden, and I will give you rest. Take my yoke upon you, and learn of me; for I am meek and lowly in heart: and ye shall find rest unto your souls. For my yoke is easy, and my burden is light."

The atonement of Jesus Christ helps bring hope and healing. The strength of our faith in the resurrection and atonement influences how well we endure the challenges we face as we navigate the turbulent waters of life. We can take comfort in the fact there is a light that will guide us, even the lighthouse of the Lord. We can also take comfort in knowing that God will send others into our lives to assist us along the way.

CLINICAL INSIGHTS

SURVIVAL SKILLS

Years ago, a friend of mine taught me to ski. He started off with a technique called snow plowing. This involved pointing the front of my skis together in the shape of a V and painstakingly moving down the ski run. The technique was awkward and slow, and it put tremendous pressure on my knees and hips, but surprisingly, it enabled me to ski down the slope without killing myself. Since it was clear to all the more experienced skiers that I was a novice and that I was on the verge of being out of control, they judiciously stayed out of my way.

After several runs, spills, and periods of controlled terror, I achieved some level of confidence. It was at that point that my friend said, "Okay, now I'm going to teach you how to really ski, so forget all you've learned so far!" He then proceeded to teach me how to keep my skis parallel, to bend my knees, and to turn my skis to control my direction and speed.

I remember thinking, *This doesn't feel right.* Compared to snow plowing, which admittedly I had little control over, I now had no control at all! I immediately went back to snow plowing. Real skiing was out of my comfort zone. From my point of view, there were no other options. Compared to the discomfort of letting go of the old ways and rising to a higher level, I decided that the pain, misery, and limitations of snow plowing weren't so bad after all. I held on to that kind of thinking until it finally became too painful to continue, which it eventually did. Then—and only then—did I finally learn to ski.

This is the same with all survival skills. We don't change them until it hurts too much not to. The Law of Accommodation states that what life requires, it creates. In other words, when we are repeatedly confronted with increasing periods of instability and mind-boggling confusion, a variety of survival skills materialize.

Emotional numbness, denial, avoidance, and isolation serve to protect us. A rigid defensiveness makes it difficult to even consider new information. When we're used to thinking wrong, what's really right seems wrong. Initially, that's why a change in thinking patterns will not change the way you feel. Recovery takes time.

Survival skills seem to be a logical attempt to cope with an illogical situation. No one really chooses these patterns beforehand. They just appear. Because they are developed in the midst of crisis situations, they become inextricably linked to, and require a continuation of, additional crisis situations. Life literally becomes nothing but one crisis after another. As a result, we tend to believe that we are really a combination of being broken, unlovable, abandoned, victimized, confused, and maybe even crazy.

When we're raised in an environment of instability and pain, we tend to accept these variables as normal, inevitably trusting the dysfunction and hesitating to let it go. The abnormal becomes normal, despair becomes reality, and the perception of helplessness and hopelessness creates the illusion that this is as good as it gets.

The ultimate goal in recovery is not to change yourself or anyone else. It's to make new choices that are more successful than those previous. When we make new choices, changes will occur on their own.

Big changes will not occur all at once but will come in bits and pieces. We only change what hurts. Until it hurts long enough and hard enough that we can't ignore it, numb it, or run from it, we tolerate it—because we really don't know how to change it to start with. That's not an excuse. That's just the way it is.

Crossing the boundaries of belief and going beyond the paralysis of fear and anxiety are difficult. Life is filled with a wide variety of choices, so live your life in such a manner that you always have a choice. If you don't recognize your ability to choose, you will lose that ability by defaulting to poor choices.

It appears that this world is accomplishing the purpose for which it was created. It's full of joys and sorrows, successes and failures. This opposition prepares us to withstand the storms of life, those we're experiencing now and those yet to come. The challenges we're facing now are simply part of the preparation for us to handle the bigger ones that will come—and come they will. That's what life is all about—growing, experiencing, and rising above our previous self. There really is a purpose to life, and there really are reasons behind opposition.

The painful elements in life—such as fear, anger, and sorrow—are things that we all try to avoid. In fact, sometimes we're so successful at avoiding them that we never develop the life-management skills necessary to cope with them, so we continue to be victimized by them.

Ironically, these painful elements are some of the integral components in the equation of life. Instead of running from them, make the attempt to face them and embrace them—both for the lessons they teach and for the strengths they give you. Take charge of your survival skills!

UNCHANGING PRINCIPLES

As the years come and go, a natural change occurs, and we invariably become either our warmest friend or our greatest enemy. In either case, given our limited knowledge, vision, and experience, it is clear that we are usually doing the best we can at any given point in time.

If we could do more, we would, and in the future we will! We're stronger today than we were yesterday, and tomorrow we'll be even stronger than today.

In this manner, we determine not only our destinies but also the very essence of our existence. This is where perception becomes so important; in spite of the people or situations in our lives, our perception is the most important factor in determining who we are now and who we will be in the future.

To paraphrase the philosopher Goethe: "When we see ourselves as we are, we make ourselves worse than we are. But when we see ourselves as if we were already in the process of achieving what we are capable of, we make ourselves what we should be."[1]

Unfortunately, worry and complacency often complicate things. Where worry creates tension and stress, complacency creates lack of tension and stress. This is where the problems begin.

On the one hand, we often worry about things that are beyond our ability to control. When we do so, we become dysfunctional. Sometimes we can become skilled at being dysfunctional.

On the other hand, complacency's message is just the opposite of worry. It's one of satisfaction with things as they are and rejection of things as they might be. "Good enough" becomes the acceptable standard. When we are complacent, we avoid the unknown, mistrust the untried, and abhor the new. In this manner, worry and complacency go hand in hand.

The solution seems to be fairly simple: learn from the past, but don't get lost in it. Plan for the future, but don't become preoccupied with it. Live only one day at a time, but live each day to the fullest.

In the midst of all the confusion and uncertainty, take consolation from the fact that it's possible to adjust to changing times and still adhere to unchanging principles. Such principles are like the lighthouse in the story about a battleship that was at sea during bad weather. The captain was on the bridge. It was foggy. Just after dark, the lookout spotted a light on the starboard side. The captain asked if it was steady or moving. The lookout replied the light was steady meaning they were on direct collision course with that ship. The captain ordered the lookout to signal to the other ship. "Change course twenty degrees. We are on a collision course." The signal came back: "Advisable for you to change course." The captain signaled, "I am a captain. Change course twenty degrees." "I am a seaman second class. You had better change course twenty degrees," came the reply. The captain was furious. He sent back, "I am a battleship. Change course!" Back came the signal, "I am a lighthouse." The captain changed course.

The captain had a choice. Fortunately, for him and his crew, he chose a course that led to safety. We too have a choice. We can choose to understand and adhere to unchanging principles or we can choose a different path. Ultimately we discover that real peace and happiness in life come as we seek to learn what they are and then live them!

THE BENEFITS OF CONFUSION

Leo Rosten has written, "In some way, however, small and secret, each of us is a little mad. . . . Happiness comes only when we push our brains out and our hearts to the farthest reaches of which we are capable."[2] What does this mean for us? First, it means that no one has all the pieces of the puzzle put together perfectly. Life is a challenge for each of us. Second, happiness only comes from putting ourselves into motion, taking all that we have known and experienced, and choosing to grow beyond where we were.

The way we choose to see the world creates the world we choose to see. In essence, we create our reality by choosing our beliefs. We are the deciding factor in defining both ourselves and the world we live in. Regardless of the pain and problems inflicted upon us, and in spite of the fairness or unfairness we encounter in life, we ultimately choose how we interpret and respond to this world.

Eventually we learn what Viktor Frankl must have meant when he wrote that the greatest of all human freedoms is the ability to choose our attitude in spite of the overwhelming situations and circumstances we encounter.[3] This may sound confusing for those who have been immobilized with or overwhelmed by the challenges of life. In reality, when we exercise the responsibility to choose our attitude, it prevents the negativity of confusion from dominating our feelings. As this change in perception settles in, we begin to see the world from a different point of view. The negative becomes more positive. The pessimistic becomes more optimistic.

It would appear that there is purpose in confusion and design in imperfection. Because of these dynamics and the discomfort that results from them, we are forced into reorganizing the way we look at the world. We are encouraged to go beyond our old comfort zones, to think outside the box in terms of perception and personal expectations, and to recognize we're not defined by our weaknesses, our mental illnesses, our family dysfunctions, or our culture. We begin to understand that we're part of something much bigger than we may have previously understood and there really is purpose and reason and wisdom in life.

There is meaning in distraction and value in irregularity. Unless we are confronted with problems that distract us, we tend to follow the path of least resistance, allowing our old, limiting patterns to continue. It's only when things become irregular that we are finally able to recognize that we require a change in course.

There is correlation in turbulence and order in distortion. Correlation refers to the process of managing the instability of life in a manner that results in a reorganization of how we see ourselves. Who we really are doesn't change with time, but who we think we are is in a constant state of revision as we move from one transitional stage to another. Turbulence and distortion allow us to continually redefine ourselves throughout life. As we do this, we gain a greater understanding of who we really are.

There is benefit in turmoil and certitude in uncertainty. The combination of these dynamics enables us to develop an assurance and a certainty in this world as we gain a greater appreciation for where we fit in. It's only in facing these challenges directly that we develop the clarity to carve out a niche for ourselves. Just as water purifies itself when it's in motion, the combination of turmoil and uncertainty result in an emotional cleansing process.

We can find orchestration in disorder and understanding in aberration. Life cannot become boring and colorless—not with the great abundance of disorder and aberration that we consistently encounter. It keeps us on our toes and reminds us that nothing in life should be taken for granted, because things seldom ever remain the same. Just about the time that we get ourselves organized and think we're one step ahead of the game, our house of cards invariably comes tumbling down.

Fortunately, no type of confusion is ever wasted. Confusion forces us to redefine what we really believe and to stretch beyond our old comfort zones. Once stretched, the discomfort of confusion encourages us to never return to our original dimensions.

Eventually, confusion illuminates, simplifies, and clarifies. When we understand and appreciate it, confusion enables us to rise above our previously accepted levels of infirmity and deficiency. The key is to recognize confusion for what it is and not be overwhelmed by what it appears to be.

NOTES

1.   Johann Wolfgang von Goethe, accessed October 10, 2011, http://www.goodreads.com/quotes/33242.

2.   Leo Rosten, Winston Churchill-Leadership, http://www.freepress.net/note/40764 (accessed Dec. 12, 2011).

3.   Viktor E. Frankl, *Man's Search for Meaning* (New York: Simon & Schuster), 75.

CHAPTER 6

EMOTIONAL RESILIENCY

I LOVE THE OLD TESTAMENT STORY OF JOSEPH IN ANCIENT Egypt. It's a story about resiliency. Joseph faced many overwhelming challenges, yet his faith in God, with the support of others, helped sustain him during difficult times.

As the story goes, some of Joseph's brothers wanted to kill him, but Reuben, the oldest brother, convinced them not to; instead, they sold Joseph to a caravan of passing Ishmaelites. These slave traders took him into Egypt and sold him to Potiphar, one of the Pharaoh's officers. Joseph served his master well and gained great favor. However, Potiphar's wife tried to seduce him. After he rejected her, she went to her husband with false accusations. It resulted in Joseph's imprisonment. Before long, the prison keeper befriended him and learned of Joseph's divine ability to interpret dreams.

Joseph was eventually called upon to interpret a dream that deeply troubled the Pharaoh. As a result of his successful interpretation, the Pharaoh rewarded him with overseeing the lands of Egypt. In these prosperous times, he stored up the abundant harvest toward the difficult times ahead. During the years of famine, Joseph's brothers came in search of grains and foods to keep their people from starvation. Not recognizing their young Hebrew brother as this prominent Egyptian leader, he ordered them to return with their younger brother. When the brothers returned with Benjamin, Joseph revealed his identity. The brothers suffered from great remorse because of their mistreatment of Joseph. Nevertheless, he chose to forgive them.

What a tremendous story of faith and resilience. Faith in God, combined with the encouragement and support of others, can also sustain us during challenging times.

As a teenager, I carefully observed coaches, teachers, and others in order to develop a sense of my own identity. Because of his own struggles, my father was usually emotionally or physically unavailable. He struggled to be a father and didn't seem to enjoy spending time with us. We learned at an early age not to share personal matters and problems with him because our sharing inevitably resulted in his becoming angry and taking it out on our mother. He simply didn't have the emotional resources to assist us in facing the challenges of our youth.

As a result, I found myself looking to other men for guidance in becoming a good husband and father. Fortunately, I was blessed with a caring youth leader who seemed to take an interest in me. Or, perhaps, I took an active interest in him because of the lack of positive adult male attention I received in the home.

He served as my Scoutmaster and coach. He supported me throughout my scouting experience and ensured that I obtained the Eagle Scout rank advancement. He coached our Little League baseball teams, and, when he wasn't coaching, he made a special effort to attend my games.

While I was in junior high and high school, he continued attending my sporting events. When he spotted me at church, he would compliment me on my performance and check to see how I was doing in school and other areas of my life. When I turned seventeen, he helped me find my first job.

Later in life, other good men became my role models. I'm grateful for the positive influence of these men and their willingness to assist someone who desperately needed their support. I also appreciated their examples and advice and didn't always wait for them to come to me, but often sought them out for guidance.

Children and youth growing up in troubled families are blessed through the nurturing relationships of caring adults. As they actively seek out and receive support, they become more emotionally resilient. They become aware of what a healthy relationship with an adult is like, and the emotional void inside of them is filled with feelings of hope and love.

Whether young or old, we can all choose to exercise faith and seek after and obtain the support we need to heal emotionally. As we do, it allows us to begin to understand the nature of a loving God, learn to put our trust in him, and grow spiritually.

CLINICAL INSIGHTS

HOW DO YOU DEFINE YOURSELF?

Usually when people are consistently unhappy, their unhappiness has more to do with how they define themselves than with what their specific problems are. Whether weak or strong, capable or incapable, secure or insecure, we tend to perceive ourselves in certain ways and then support those perceptions with beliefs and behaviors that anchor us in that level of development. In reality, our perceptions about ourselves are merely a belief system that we choose to accept. So if you don't like the way you've defined yourself up until now, make new choices. That's where it all begins.

As human beings, we tend to believe that we are what we believe we are. But our perceptions are only beliefs, and beliefs can be altered or discarded. It just takes practice. We also tend to believe that our past experiences are all-controlling—that simply because we've always acted in a certain way, we will always continue to act that way. But that's not true either. It's only another example of an incorrect belief system.

In life, each of us will progress at a rate that only we are capable of determining. Regardless of how encouraging or discouraging others may be, no one else is accountable for the speed with which we progress or for the pain that we bring upon ourselves because of poor choices. Fortunately, negative experiences do not exist, only experiences that serve to strengthen, develop, and clarify the person we really are. Nothing is wasted, regardless of what we have come to believe.

We must determine how to define ourselves. When it comes to our natural tendencies or predispositions, our self-made definitions are powerful. We are either the victim or the victor. Victims allow themselves to be controlled by their natural tendencies and predispositions. Victors manage them by choosing to replace their natural predispositions with a course of self-mastery, self-discipline, and reliance upon correct principles. Victors also seek out the help they need to succeed.

Self-mastery, self-discipline, reliance upon correct principles, and seeking out help are ultimately the essential building blocks of happiness. So invest in yourself. Be victorious! After all, you're exchanging a day of your life for today.

PORTALS OF DISCOVERY

If we have everything but a sense of who we really are, we have nothing. And yet, if we have nothing but a sense of who we really are, we really have everything.

Unfortunately, we sometimes get lost while trying to discover who we really are. If we can keep the big picture in mind—that we're in this world to gain experience and touch the lives of those around us—then everything else becomes manageable. In other words, we're not broken simply because we're not yet perfect.

In fact, life appears to be orchestrated in such a manner that even our weaknesses, inabilities, limitations, and disabilities enable us to touch the lives of those around us in ways that only we can. Because of their impact upon us, our problems force us to redefine ourselves. In essence, they are our portals of discovery.

I've come to believe that God is intimately involved in our life process, and that things are so well coordinated that he has already prepared others to answer prayers we haven't even prayed yet. He knows what our needs are now and he knows what they will be in the future. He has prepared others to be brought into our lives to touch our spirits, strengthen us, and fill the void that we sometimes feel. The most exciting part of this process is that you're in the midst of becoming one of these "tour guides" yourself.

The recovery process you're going through right now is much bigger than you are, and it has a much greater significance than the pain of your own personal issues. As a result of the choices you're making, changes will occur. Your life and the lives of those with whom you are involved will never be the same. With the insight, understanding, and wisdom that will develop from this experience, and with the knowledge of tools and techniques that you'll learn, you'll find solutions to your problems, and you'll be brought into the lives of others in a manner that will replenish both your energy and theirs.

We really do have a worth that is far beyond our mortal ability to fully comprehend. Because it's so far beyond us, its effect will be to serve as a guiding beacon that will quietly but most assuredly lead us home.

CREATING A NEW BELIEF IN OURSELVES

All that we've lived through and had experience with in the past has colored our perception of who and what we are in the present. But remember, it's only a perception of who we are and not who we really are. In the past, we may have felt that we had very little choice in these matters. The future is different. The future is ours, and the future starts now!

Unfortunately, because of the patterns of the past, some people believe that it is impossible to alter old belief systems. Even if it were possible to change these patterns, a unique set of conditions must be in place before these individuals would consider taking corrective measures.

The fact is that these perceptions are not immutable or unalterable, and they will transform us, but only when we are prepared to accept such changes. It's also true that we begin to believe in ourselves, even when things are difficult—not only in the sunlight, where every detail is clear and every probability has been calculated, but also in the dark, where uncertainty and fear serve as the incentives that generate change. This change triggers a developmental process that results in new experiences; new experiences lead to expansion; expansion leads to confidence; and confidence leads to clarity. Such a process is never easy, but it's always worth it. These principles serve as a foundation for a new reality, and they allow natural laws to form the basis of this new perception. In this manner, a new future will begin to rise from the ashes of the painful past.

As a result, we begin to realize that we can be the choice we wish to make. We can become what we search for. We can create the transformation from what we were to what we are capable of becoming. We can rise above the fears that seek to immobilize us. We can progress toward what we aspire to be. We can adapt to the ideals we search for. We can revise the limitations that may have controlled us. We can harness the pain and grow beyond it. We can bridle our courage to defeat uncertainty. We can formulate new methods to overcome confusion. We can attune ourselves to the positive forces in life. We can redesign our old, imperfect perception of who we are as we envision what we dream we can become. We can recruit the help of caring individuals to assist us in rising above our past. We can synchronize what we previously thought was hopelessly disorganized, and we can generate a metamorphosis that will enable us to rise to previously unexpected levels of achievement. From an eternal perspective, we can accept nothing less!

PART TWO

GROWING SPIRITUALLY

CHAPTER 7

"NOT MY WILL, BUT THINE, BE DONE"

ONE OF THE GREATEST CHALLENGES WE ALL FACE IS that of striving to know and do the will of God. At times it seems that it's far too easy to be distracted by worldly influences or just be buried by our own pain, thereby neglecting to do what matters most. We may be going through the motions, doing those things we believe would help us grow spiritually, but not fully benefiting from these activities, because our hearts may be somewhere else. We may be overly concerned with past hurts or with something else that would divert our attention from our real purpose in life. For some of us, the abuse or neglect we've experienced may have left us so hollow inside, so detached from ourselves and God, that going through the motions is all that we know.

Our insecurities, preoccupations, or addictions may even lead us to believe that the time we have here in this life is our own, to be spent in the way we deem appropriate. We may be angry with God because of our suffering. Our will gradually begins to take priority over God's will.

What does it mean to submit our will to God's? When our daughter, Lauren, was three years old she did what many children do when they discover a pair of scissors in the house—she gave herself a haircut. Lauren cut off her bangs and big chunks of hair on both sides of her head. A few days later a friend of ours—upon noticing Lauren's handiwork—jokingly commented to my wife that Lauren looked like a self-made woman.

While my wife was grocery shopping with Lauren several weeks later, a stranger approached them and said that Lauren was a cute little girl. In response, Lauren loudly proclaimed, "I am not. I'm a self-made woman!"

Certainly, as God's children we understand that we are not self-made individuals. We owe our very existence, all that we have and all that we obtain in this life, to a loving God. Therefore, it should be our lifelong goal to strive to do his will.

Humbly seeking to do what God would like us to do is challenging. I've had to work at it. On a number of occasions, I would have preferred to spend time engaged in personal interests rather than in serving others. However, I've learned that when we do what God wants us to do, everything inevitably works out the way that it should.

God loves us too much to let us be content with the level of spirituality we have achieved currently. He allows us to experience certain individualized challenges that provide us with opportunities for spiritual growth. These opportunities help us draw closer to him. How we respond to each of these challenges and opportunities largely determines the amount of spiritual growth we experience.

There is a story called "The Unwise Bee" that illustrates how we sometimes respond to life's challenges:

> A wild bee from the neighboring hills once flew into the room, and at intervals during an hour or more I caught the pleasing hum of its flight. The little creature realized that it was a prisoner, yet all its efforts to find the exit through the partly opened casement failed.
>
> When ready to close up the room and leave, I threw the window wide, and tried at first to guide and then to drive the bee to liberty and safety, knowing well that if left in the room it would die as other insects there entrapped had perished in the dry atmosphere of the enclosure. The more I tried to drive it out, the more determinedly did it oppose and resist my efforts. Its erstwhile peaceful hum developed into an angry roar; its darting flight became hostile and threatening.
>
> Then it caught me off my guard and stung my hand—the hand that would have guided it to freedom. At last it alighted on a pendant attached to the ceiling, beyond my reach of help or injury. The sharp pain of its unkind sting aroused in me rather pity than anger. I knew

the inevitable penalty of its mistaken opposition and defiance, and I had to leave the creature to its fate.

Three days later I returned to the room and found the dried, lifeless body of the bee on the writing table. It had paid for its stubbornness with its life. To the bee's short-sightedness and selfish misunderstanding I was a foe, a persistent persecutor, a mortal enemy bent on its destruction; while in truth I was its friend, offering it ransom of the life it had put in forfeit through its own error, striving to redeem it, in spite of itself, from the prison house of death and restore it to the outer air of liberty.[1]

Do we sometimes resist or even fight God's spiritual tutoring? When faced with challenges, do we humbly seek to understand and do his will or do we resist and choose to do things our way?

Obedience to God's laws and submitting to his will is vital to our happiness and to achieving our life's purpose. It helps us to draw closer to him. So then, in what ways can we demonstrate our obedience to God, or in what ways can we become more spiritually submissive? There may be others, but the following five have helped me.

1. *Serve others.* Giving meaningful service to others (for example, teaching a child at the local school to read, volunteering at the community food bank, helping an elderly neighbor with yard work, and so on) empowers us to put personal issues in perspective and learn to do God's will rather than our own.

2. *Seek learning and work hard.* Some may wonder how this relates to obedience to God's will. I think it has a lot to do with it. In my life, education and hard work were one of the keys to breaking free from the effects of abuse and related unhealthy patterns of behavior. I've discovered that lifelong learning, which also includes regularly studying the scriptures, provides lifelong answers to daily challenges. Understanding and doing God's will is not a passive process, but an active one. It requires work!

3. *Stay morally clean.* Most people who suffer from abuse may also have addictive personalities. As a result, they may easily develop other forms of addictions. In today's world, the viewing of pornography and violence, immorality, and substance abuse

are made to appear acceptable. They are not—and never will be—acceptable. They lead to addictions that destroy the ability to feel God's influence. If necessary, a qualified therapist who specializes in treating addictions can provide the support and counseling required for recovery.

4. *Cultivate a sense of humor and participate in wholesome recreational activities.* A balanced perspective about life increases our desire to do God's will. Therefore, it's important to see the humorous side of things. Good humor helps put our daily challenges in perspective.

    According to Allen Klein, author of *The Healing Power of Humor*, "In laughter, we transcend our predicaments. We are lifted above our feelings of fear, discouragement, and despair."[2] Good humor enables us to experience positive emotions, neutralize negative emotions, and to not take ourselves too seriously which can help keep us on the path to greater happiness.

    In addition, wholesome recreational activities help us to appreciate the beauty in the world around us. Like humor, recreational activities provide us with perspective, balance, and enjoyment—all of which are especially important for individuals who have experienced emotional trauma. Even in ancient Greece, the preferred treatment for individuals struggling with emotional challenges was to require that they attend theatrical comedies.

5. *Show love and respect toward family members.* We must learn to forgive and let go of any anger we may feel toward a family member and work to replace it with love.

We each need to draw nearer to God by letting go of anything that would impede our ability to grow spiritually. This includes sacrificing our obsessions, addictions, and other dysfunctions on the Lord's altar and replacing fear with faith and love.

CLINICAL INSIGHTS

WHEN LIFE BECOMES OUT OF FOCUS

Several years ago, my family and I were preparing to go on a short vacation to St. George, Utah. It was the middle of the winter, just after Christmas in 1994. Everything was packed and ready to go when I realized we didn't have our old video camera. I mentioned that fact to my wife and headed into the house to look for it. "It won't do any good to bring it along," she said. "It's broken. I got it out a few weeks ago, and it looked like someone had dropped it. Everything is out of focus."

I found it in the closet, brought it down for an examination, and sure enough, everything was out of focus. I yelled out the front door, "This thing really is out of focus!" I couldn't see her reaction, but I knew she was shaking her head and biting her tongue to keep from saying something she would regret. "Maybe I can fix it," I said.

Now, when I begin to repair anything, the first step is always the same. It begins with the same scientific precision I use when I kick the tire of a car to ascertain its quality. I began to shake the camera and bang it with my hand. And to no one's surprise, it remained out of focus.

Then I looked at the twenty-five buttons on the camera, pushed five or six of them, and still it was out of focus. Then I remembered I had bought an extended warranty, so I called the store. Sure enough, the warranty had expired three months before. So there I was with a broken camera, buttons that didn't do anything, a warranty that wouldn't help, and no one in particular who I could blame. I was just about to throw the whole thing in the trash can when I noticed a small knob on the viewfinder. I turned it a fraction of an inch and everything came into focus. The camera itself wasn't broken. It was just out of focus.

I triumphantly walked out to the van where everyone was waiting impatiently for me and casually stated, "I fixed it." Silence radiated from every open mouth in the van, and I drove off with the quiet confidence of a man who creates miracles every day.

The point of this story is that in life things often appear broken beyond repair. Individuals, relationships, families, and even society may fall into this category. Mistakes and problems appear too big to tackle, and we often feel overwhelmed. But many times things aren't broken—they're just out of focus.

The lens on a camera can be compared to the way we see the world around us, or our perception. Based on our perception, we make certain interpretations of our reality. You have to remember that our perception is our reality, regardless of what others may think and regardless of how accurate or inaccurate that perception may be. According to our interpretation of our perception, we change certain behaviors that are not in balance with our perception. And based on the behaviors we choose, we make some kind of impact on the world. If the impact is positive, the behavioral choices are reinforced, supporting the fact that our interpretation is accurate and our perception is correct. However, when the impact is negative, it indicates that something is out of balance. It could be us, or it could be the world around us, and at times it's really difficult to know which.

When our perception is inaccurate, a natural set of laws kicks in. First, the rules for living that we've accepted no longer seem to work consistently. As a result, we become unable to satisfactorily identify and meet our needs. One of our most important needs is to love and be loved. This need can even make the difference between life and death for newborn children. Newborns that don't receive sufficient love have a higher mortality rate. Children and youth who don't receive much-needed love and attention in their homes may begin to search for it elsewhere, and they usually search in the wrong places.

When adults feel this void where love should be, it's not uncommon that they try to fill it with something else. All too frequently, this turns into an addiction of some sort, and there are many types of addictions. The one thing they all have in common is that they end in pain.

We have a tremendous need to have positive self-esteem and to feel good about ourselves. When we rely on incorrect principles to achieve this sense of worth, we set ourselves up for disappointment and unhappiness. Sooner or later, we're going to look in the mirror and see something that we don't like. Despite the façade we've created to make ourselves appear well to others, we usually know who we really are inside. We can only hide behind this image for so long. Eventually, others see through it. Sadly, some of us go through life scared to death, thinking someone will discover that we're a fake or a fool deep down.

We typically need to have someone in our lives who thinks we're important and who loves us. This tends to motivate us to rise above mediocrity. It also allows us to shift our attention away from ourselves and become less self-centered in the process. Some, however, develop the idea that they are inadequate by themselves. As a result, they may become dependent on others for their sense of worth.

We also need variety. Without it, life becomes dull, boring, and mundane. Life loses its color, and everything becomes black and white. At that point, the goal is merely to survive, and we are no longer able to seek variety.

Another major need is control. We seem to have a basic instinct when it comes to control: we either take control or delegate it to others. In either case, unless we manage control effectively, we lose it completely.

It's important to remember that bad things happen to good people on a regular basis. Bad things are unavoidable and apparently necessary. The experience we get from managing these struggles forces us to grow and develop, even when that's not what we think we want or need. With this in mind, the most important thing is not what happens to us but what we do with what happens to us.

During these periods of trial and frustration, one of the most critical tools in managing them effectively is to keep the big picture in mind. This is where faith, hope, patience, humility, and sincere prayer are especially helpful. If we use these tools, we will tend not to be as easily overwhelmed as we might otherwise be. These attributes will help us see how certain problems and challenges are the necessary components for this phase of our journey through life.

If we don't have this "big picture" perspective in mind, we must work to develop it. Some of the key strategies to help us maintain perspective include the following areas:

1. *Physical.* This entails doing what is necessary to maintain good health. A balanced diet, plenty of sleep, and daily exercise are essential for a healthy lifestyle. It's about self-care. We simply can't get so busy that we don't take time to "sharpen the saw."

2. *Social/emotional.* Family, friends, church, and community involvement fall into this area. While it's necessary that we develop ourselves as individuals, we function best when we

are able to contribute to something larger than ourselves; it's important for us to find opportunities to serve and love others. What makes this difficult to achieve is that to contribute in any significant way, we must be able to see our fundamental self-worth first.

3. *Mental.* In this life, a good education is the key to opportunity! It's the great equalizer. There is power in learning, and we can transcend our past by learning about ourselves, others, and the world around us. Learning is an essential part of our eternal progression.

4. *Spiritual.* An understanding of our relationship to God is vital. By ourselves, we are limited and finite. As we come to identify and understand our own limitations and our need for God's assistance, we are able to tap into the infinite. After all, it has been said that we're not mortal beings having spiritual experiences, but spiritual beings having mortal experiences.[3] To achieve the ultimate spiritual success during this life, we must have patience and refinement. While we seldom obtain all of the spiritual affirmation and confirmation that we want, we usually receive what we need. When we receive what we need, we'll find it was just what we wanted all along.

5. *Financial.* We often fail to fully appreciate this part of the equation. Unless we learn to manage finances effectively, financial problems can have a negative and sometimes devastating effect on all other needs. This is where planning, preparation, and performance are essential.

In essence, the development of a big-picture perspective is really the development of an eternal perspective that allows us to manage our destiny. Balance is the key. As long as we keep the components mentioned above in balance, the odds are that we'll be relatively happy.

However, too many people allow exterior influences in their lives to control their thoughts, choices, and behaviors. Things get out of balance. Granted, certain things in life are beyond our control. We must learn to accept them as they are and learn to manage them before they manage us. Other things in life can be controlled effectively, as long as we don't give up too soon. With this in mind, happiness in life seems to come from understanding the Serenity Prayer: "God grant me the serenity to accept the things I cannot change, courage to change the things I can, and wisdom to know the difference." Our life does not need to be out of focus. It can be filled with a clear vision of what matters most.

UNHAPPINESS IS NOT AN ACCIDENT

When we do what must be done, our confidence and self-mastery will expand. But when we allow fear or confusion to control us, unhappiness will result. When we work through life's challenges, our anxiety will decrease and our peace of mind will increase. But when we become immobilized by self-doubt, unhappiness will result.

When we are of service to those around us, a sense of significance will develop, but when we begin to feel responsible for everyone and everything, unhappiness will result. When we give of ourselves, we will develop greater skills and depth, but when we do so with an ulterior motive, unhappiness will result.

When we fight the battles that must be fought, we will develop greater strength and resilience, but when we try to run from these battles or avoid them at all costs, unhappiness will result. When we risk reaching out to others, our fears will diminish and our insight will increase, but when we allow our fears to overwhelm us, unhappiness will result.

When we commit ourselves to the higher road, our clarity will increase and discipline will expand our abilities, but when we settle for mediocrity, unhappiness will result. When we appreciate the beauty that surrounds us, we will find an optimism that will help us manage difficult times, but when we ignore the beauty or take it for granted, unhappiness will result.

When we face the problems that intimidate us, our reassurance and determination will flourish, but if we merely tolerate the pain, we will become victimized by it, and unhappiness will result. When we grow beyond where we've been, we will discover characteristics and abilities that we may not have recognized before, but if we fail to initiate this growth process, unhappiness will result.

Unfortunately, with enough time and practice, unhappiness can occur so frequently and our perception can become so distorted that we may actually begin to see unhappiness as normal. We cannot afford this type of self-betrayal. Therefore, it's critical that we strive to discover and understand the forces that seek to control our lives. Discovering and understanding these forces are the first steps toward learning to manage them, and to fail to recognize them is to empower these forces to continue expanding. We must also recognize and alter the patterns of behavior that have immobilized us in the past. This, in turn, enables us to rise above them. However, to allow these patterns to continue uninterrupted is to sanction the pain and unhappiness they leave in their wake.

Finally, to envision and formulate a new-and-improved version of ourselves is to generate a new and necessary version of reality. But to falter in this responsibility is to undermine our happiness and fail to appreciate our inherent worth. Designing and accepting a new perception of ourselves is a prerequisite to emancipation and liberation. If we fail to do what we know must be done for our own improvement, we incapacitate the natural laws that can carry out this miraculous transformation.

EVERYTHING IS ALREADY ALL RIGHT

It may sound cliché, but if what you're doing isn't giving you what you want, then don't do it anymore. Life is a long journey, and you probably aren't done yet, so be patient with yourself and learn to enjoy the ride. Believe it or not, life is not a life-threatening illness! I've come to believe that everything is going to turn out all right. If I really believe that everything is going to turn out all right, then I have to accept the fact that everything is already all right. There is a divinely orchestrated plan that uses pain and frustration to teach us, reach us, and prepare us for what's to come. In essence, we are being prepared today for what's going to happen ten years down the road. This preparation never ends but continues throughout life.

No one escapes this process. Though our trials may vary, we will never become immune to them—no immunity from the pain or loss or difficulties brought on by our own mistakes and no immunity from the confusion or insanity brought on by the actions of others. Sometimes it almost seems to be too much to bear, but it's not. Life wasn't meant to be accommodating and pain free, but it wasn't meant to be so overwhelming that we would give up.

To manage life effectively and to achieve some measure of happiness, we need to do three things. First, we need to develop an eternal perspective that helps us see the light at the end of the tunnel. Second, we need to accept ourselves as we are right now, with the expectation that we're going to continue to grow. And third, we need to be willing to forgive both ourselves and others.

If a seed doesn't grow, it dies. When it does grow, it eventually destroys its old container and must be transplanted in a new pot. Growth can be painful. I guess that's why we tend to avoid it. However, happiness requires a combination of discovery and growth. If we're not committed to these principles, we will be hesitant, anxious, and ineffective.

Happiness is a by-product that occurs naturally as we discover and accept who we are, and as we become who we are meant to become. This process continues to repeat itself as we move from one level of development to the next.

As we master each new level of development, we develop a greater emotional depth that enables us to reduce our dependence on people, situations, or circumstances. Happiness is an integral part of this development. Happiness is having options, alternatives, and choices, not addiction, dependency, or domination. Happiness is developing an optimistic perception in which our focus is on the rose, not on the thorn.

Since some people weren't raised to be happy, they don't expect to be happy. They deprive themselves of the happiness and pleasures in this world, clinging to the idea that, in the eternities, they will have it all. Now, while that may be true, we need to remember that we're in the midst of eternity now. Eternity is not something that's going to happen in the future. It's here and it's now. It's okay to be happy!

We exist for a reason, and it seems clear that happiness should be a part of that existence. We have a right to be happy. However, with every right comes a responsibility to ourselves and to those around us. With every responsibility comes an obligation, and with every obligation, a duty. Each of us must define these variables as we define ourselves. A systematic, disciplined approach is necessary to put life back in balance for those who have been used, abused, or confused or for those who suffer from depression or anxiety disorders. Without balance, there can be no long-term happiness.

The good news is that no one has to remain stuck in a rut. If we feel a sense of powerlessness, it can be replaced with strength and confidence. If we feel a loss of freedom, it can be replaced with choices. We can stabilize, understand, and manage our confused feelings. Since our symptoms are messages, an important question is, "What are they trying to tell us?" Part of the answer is, "Everything is already all right."

NOTES

1.   James E. Talmage, "Three Parables—The Unwise Bee, the Owl Express, and Two Lamps," *Ensign*, February 2003, 36.

2.   Allen Klein, *The Healing Power of Humor* (New York: Penguin Putman Inc., 1989), 4.

3.   Pierre Teilhard de Chardin, www.csec.org, accessed December 12, 2011, http://realtalklibrary.com. From *The Phenomenon of Man* (New York: Harper & Row, London: William Collins Sons and Company, Ltd., 1959).

CHAPTER 8

FEAR AND FAITH

"FOR GOD HATH NOT GIVEN US THE SPIRIT OF FEAR; BUT of power, and of love, and of a sound mind" (2 Timothy 1:7). At an early age, my siblings and I learned to fear what might happen to us if we said or did the wrong thing around our father. We discovered that it didn't take much to trigger his wrath. Unfinished chores, problems at school, or squabbling with siblings could result in angry tirades and family meetings, where we would spend hours together while he berated a particular family member or our mother. So in order to maintain peace, we learned not to share personal problems, to say what he wanted to hear, and to do what he wanted us to do. Whenever we varied from this standard, which was inevitable due to our young ages, we paid a price or our mother suffered. He would often say, "I'm the father" in order to justify his actions.

Not surprisingly, my mother was usually extremely anxious. Her anxiety affected all of us. If something could go wrong, she imagined it would. In her mind, a sprained ankle became a broken leg, a sore throat and cough became pneumonia, and so on. Her severe anxiety caused her to negatively fantasize about almost anything and anyone.

Unfortunately, our home was a breeding ground for fear. Outwardly, our family went through the motions by attending church and praying together; inwardly, it seemed that we had no concept of faith in God. In fact, as children we feared God the same way we feared our

CHANGE YOUR CHOICES, CHANGE YOUR LIFE

father. At times, it was extremely hard to believe that a loving God even existed because of what we experienced in our home.

Nevertheless, during my youth I took courage from reading the amazing story recorded in the Bible about Daniel in the lions' den. Daniel was thrown into the den of lions because he refused to cease his praying during the time that bowing to anyone other than the king was banned. King Darius's followers were filled with jealousy of Daniel because of his integrity and the favor he had won with the king. They went to the king and convinced him to make a decree that sentenced anyone who disobeyed it to be thrown into the lions' den. But when Daniel discovered that the decree had been published, he went home to his upstairs room where the windows opened toward Jerusalem. Three times a day he knelt down and prayed, giving thanks to his God, just as he had done before.

Not long thereafter, King Darius's followers reported his disobedience. But when the king heard that he had disobeyed him, he was in great distress. He wanted to save Daniel but was bound by the law that he had decreed.

Hence, the king gave the order, Daniel was thrown into the lions' den. The king was restless throughout the night, and at the first light of dawn, he hurried to the lions' den to inquire of Daniel whether his God had saved him. To the king's great surprise, Daniel answered, "O king, live for ever. My God hath sent his angel, and hath shut the lions' mouths, that they have not hurt me" (Daniel 6:21–22).

Daniel understood the source of his strength. His faith in God helped him to manage and overcome his fears.

Over the years, I've discovered that fear increases, rather than decreases, as we choose to do our will rather than God's will—whether we do so in response to a painful past or what we perceive to be a frightful future. Because of severe emotional—and in some instances physical—pain, many individuals who have lived in abusive environments find it extremely difficult, if not impossible, to enjoy the present. As adults, we continue to focus on past hurts. We also tend to worry excessively about the future. The anxiety, fear, and despair that come from such thinking can be debilitating. For some, professional assistance may be the only way to obtain relief from these thoughts.

We know the adversary seeks to introduce fear into our lives, but faith in God and following Christ's example will help us to overcome it, and I conclude as I began, "For God hath not given us the spirit of fear; but of power, and of love, and of a sound mind" (2 Timothy 1:7).

CLINICAL INSIGHTS

OUR FIELD OF VISION

Life appears to be an orchestrated process in which we eventually discover that the best of times and the worst of times are not really measures of our success or failure but are tests that teach certain lessons and instill certain principles. Two of the most important of these principles are faith and fear. Ultimately, we build a life on these principles. We decide which principle will overcome the other within our own lives.

If we live a life based primarily upon fear, then we relegate ourselves to a self-imposed prison. Our field of vision narrows, and anxiety becomes our universe. As a result, we may literally become incapable of appreciating the beauty of the sunrise because we have become immobilized by the darkness of the night. If we choose to live a life based primarily on faith (for example faith in God and faith in natural laws), then our field of vision expands and becomes a powerful influence with an intense clarity that serves as the foundation of our freedom.

Because of faith, we can be confident that one of two things will happen when we are about to step off into the great abyss of darkness and uncertainty. Either we'll find stepping-stones that have been uniquely prepared for us to find and that will lead us to higher levels, or we'll find that there are no stepping-stones, and we'll learn to fly!

When we consciously decide on a faith-based philosophy of life, many benefits will manifest, but none of them will immunize us from the pain and problems that are a natural and necessary part of our existence. Instead, this philosophy of faith will generate something of even greater significance—peace of mind. When we have peace of mind, we don't need much else. But if we don't have it, then it doesn't really matter what else we do have.

Without faith, our perception can become so easily distorted that we may settle for less than what we are capable of becoming. That is why it's so important to remember that we are not just human "beings," we are human "becomings." We're not done yet! That is probably what Shakespeare meant when he wrote the lines, "We know what we are, but know not what we may be."[1] Life is filled with a series of cycles that are designed to help us progress to higher levels. While uncertainty is a natural part of this process, the uncertainty won't last forever. The key to success in this endeavor is to move as fearlessly as possible from one cycle to the next, strengthening our faith, remembering who we are, expanding our field of vision, integrating the lessons learned, and being grateful for the opportunity to do so.

TIME

Everything changes with time. As we make it through changes, we usually discover that we're larger than our pain and fears, that we're stronger than our weaknesses, and that we're more significant than our feelings of emptiness. In essence, time is the great sculptor of our lives. It's a force that changes us from the inside out. It's a power that calms the uncertainty, and, like a friend, time forces us to learn lessons that only time can teach.

As these truths distill upon our minds, the result is a gentle reminder that we are part of something much greater than ourselves. With this insight comes a heightened awareness of a responsibility that can only be described as love. That which we love, we become, so that which we love defines who we are. Where we are now, at this point in our development, is important. But what we will become is so much more than what we are now. We have to believe it to see it. It is only once we believe in our divine potential that we ever have a chance to reach it. Love is the eternal thread that has been woven into the tapestry of our lives.

Like the ebb and flow of the tide, time passes and change occurs. For some, the constant change in life results in peaceful acceptance, and for others it causes only hesitancy and anxiety. Some look forward to growing and developing, and others resist—not only because of their old fears but also because change of any kind can be intimidating. They convince themselves they can't change, or shouldn't change, because they're broken. They rigidly hold on to this point of view even when it causes pain. They tend to believe that their feelings are facts and that their perceptions are accurate. Consequently, they tend to settle for "getting by" rather than "getting well." In some cases, they believe they deserve nothing better.

Fortunately, change occurs in spite of our best efforts to avoid it, culminating in the potentially curative effects of a breakdown. Without a breakdown, there is rarely a breakthrough. For some, that's what it takes. Rules change. Lives change. Hearts change. Sometimes, even we change.

NOTES

1.   Shakespeare, *Hamlet*, act 4, scene 5, accessed December 14, 2011, http://www.shakespeare-literature.com/hamlet/16.html.

CHAPTER 9

FOLLOW CHRIST

THE PROCESS OF FOLLOWING CHRIST IS JUST THAT, A process. We sometimes become impatient with ourselves and others as we participate in this process. It's easy to become frustrated and to feel unworthy due to unhealthy patterns of behavior we've developed over the years. Or we may have the tendency to judge others in an attempt to "remove the mote in our brother's eye" (see Luke 6:42). Both practices can harm and prevent our spiritual growth. Hence, we must each learn to exercise patience, long-suffering, gentleness, meekness, and love for ourselves and others as we participate in this process.

To focus on our own or others' past mistakes, sins, or abuses limits our ability to develop Christlike attributes. We deny the miraculous influence of the atonement when we fail to access its power to help us overcome the effects of abuse and other unhealthy patterns of behavior. The atonement not only benefits the sinner, but also those victims who have been sinned against. Forgiveness is essential for continued spiritual progress.

God knows our potential. He clearly sees what we can become. That is why he gives us commandments—to help us grow, to move us in the direction we need to go, and to help us realize our potential.

As a husband and father, I've benefited greatly from striving to follow Christ's example and live his teachings. Yet throughout this process I've also made my share of mistakes.

For example, throughout my youth I was always extremely competitive when it came to sports. I believe that part of my competitiveness was due to the intense anger I felt toward my father. Sports were a productive and therapeutic outlet. I was aggressive on the basketball court and mild-mannered everywhere else.

After getting married and having children, I found that my competitive spirit persisted. I wanted my oldest son to have the same positive experiences I had playing sports as a boy. I wanted him to excel so he could enjoy the experience of winning, which meant everything to me as a young man. It seemed that my ego, or sense of worth and confidence, were derived from my skills as an athlete.

After one particularly close baseball game when our son was about ten years old, I remember how frustrated I was with him—not only because his team had lost but also because I felt he wasn't playing up to his potential. He just didn't seem to have the same level of intensity and drive I had as a boy. The thought crossed my mind that my father never spent time teaching me how to play sports and helping me to develop my athletic skills. How could my son not perform the way he should when I had spent more time with him than my father had spent with me?

That evening upon returning home from his game, my frustration got the best of me, and I verbally expressed it to him. I displayed little understanding or love in my critique of his performance. Needless to say I hurt his feelings. I was sorry but too proud to say so.

The next morning as I was preparing for work, I found a note from my son on my bed. In his note, he expressed how much he loved and admired me and how much my words hurt him. He asked that I try a little harder to be patient and understanding with him as he worked to become a better baseball player.

My heart sunk after reading his note. I immediately went into his bedroom and hugged him. I apologized, expressed my sincere love, and told him I would try harder to be patient in the future. He taught me a valuable lesson about the need to exercise patience and understanding for him as he developed his skills as a young baseball player.

Of course, becoming skilled at sports is far less important than becoming skilled at following Christ. While being successful on the playing field may bring short-term rewards, being successful at living the Christian life brings eternal ones. The important point to remember is that exercising love, patience, and understanding for ourselves and others throughout the process of becoming is essential for our progress.

Following Christ is a lifelong process. At times we may feel a bit overwhelmed as we struggle to follow him. We can take comfort in knowing that God knows each of us individually. He understands our needs and desires perfectly, and he lightens our burdens and blesses us as we make our journey through life. God will patiently and lovingly help us manage our weaknesses, magnify our strengths, overcome our sins and other personal challenges, and eventually, we will experience a change of heart.

God's help often comes through the loving support of others. Throughout this process, we must strive to show patience and love for ourselves and for those he sends into our lives to assist us.

CLINICAL INSIGHTS

SELF-LOVE

A Pharisee approached the Savior and asked, "Master, which is the great commandment in the law? Jesus said unto him, Thou shalt love the Lord thy god with all they heart, and with all thy soul, and with all thy mind. This is the first and great commandment. And the second is like unto it, Thou shalt love thy neighbor as thyself" (Matthew 22:36–39).

Unless we are able to love ourselves, it's extremely difficult to love our neighbor. The topic of self-love is commonly misunderstood. In my opinion, recognizing the value of self-love is as important as understanding power, control, agency, and the purpose of life experiences. I'm convinced that God wants us to have a wide variety of experiences. He wants us to make good use of our ability to choose. He wants us to understand power and control so that we may learn to manage them. I'm convinced that he wants us to develop self-love. While all of these things can be misused and abused, we must understand and master each of them if we are to become like the Savior. So what attributes do we have that we should love? I assume it has something to do with self-worth.

"What is man, that thou art mindful of him? . . . For thou hast made him a little lower than the angels, and hast crowned him with glory and honour. Thou madest him to have dominion over the works of thy hands; thou hast put all things under his feet" (Psalm 8:4–6). I think God has great plans for us.

The following scripture provides us with further enlightenment concerning our worth: "I will make a man more precious than fine gold" (Isaiah 13:12).

I believe God really cares for us. He created us. He loves us perfectly and is willing to give us all that he has. Because he loves us, we should also love ourselves. Self-love is a normal and necessary part of our eternal development.

As our capacity for self-love increases, a transformation takes place. We develop greater emotional maturity. We become more centered, more balanced, and more accepting. We make fewer demands on others, and we develop an ability to rise above our own concerns. As others see this, they will be drawn to us, and our relationships will develop greater depth and substance. From everything that I've been taught, it is clear that God wants us to be successful in this endeavor.

It appears that our fate, or our destiny, is nothing but a natural set of laws that God uses to influence our lives. Throughout history, philosophers have written that destiny is the result of character, character is the result of habit, and habit is the result of choice. From this point of view, destiny is not a matter of chance—it's a matter of choice. God is the author of choice.

Through our agency, or our choices, we become who we are capable of being. God's love and our own self-love are major elements in this process. Hence, we will not fail. However, many of us will progress slowly. And while this process is not always easy, I'm convinced that it's manageable.

We all have the tendency to see ourselves through a clouded lens. We get all mixed up with our past, our fears, and our pain. We are not our past, although we are touched by it. We are not our fear, although we are drawn to it, and we are not our pain, although we develop because of it. These are some of the essential steps in the development of self-love.

During the process of developing self-love, we eventually realize that we determine our personal limits, our interpersonal boundaries, and the expectations that we set for ourselves and for others. It's a process of learning how to love ourselves and others.

Our interpersonal boundaries include being able to set healthy limits with others, establishing healthy life-management skills, and setting realistic expectations that provide balance, stability, and control. Each of these is directly related to self-love.

In fact, the following three concepts form the basis of our reality. We can only accomplish what we think we can. We can only become what we think we are. We can only be what we repeatedly do.

God understands this. That's why this world was created specifically for us. Because of his plan, our problems were never meant to be permanent, our mistakes were never meant to destroy, and our patterns of behavior were never meant to stop our progression. These things were meant to serve as a foundation for learning, for building upon, and for rising above. I believe that God wants us to know what lies behind us and what lies before us but that he wants us to know what lies within us even more.

We didn't come into this world to obtain self-worth—we brought it with us. Because we've always had it, our job is not to develop it but to discover it. Self-love is directly tied to this. Ultimately, we are the deciding factor in the discovery of self-love. In essence, we have to believe it to see it.

This is a beautiful world, and—no doubt—it is accomplishing the purpose for which it was created. We're primarily here to learn to be like Jesus. Fortunately, it's never too late to start our process of change. Embracing that process is what self-love is all about. Giving us that opportunity is what God's love is all about. We must learn for ourselves that we are worthy to have both our own self-love and his love.

CHOICE AND ACCOUNTABILITY

Apparently, life is as it is. Sometimes it's simple, and sometimes it's confusing. In either case, it appears that our choices are the determining factor in managing every part of life. Because of this natural law, we are 100 percent successful in achieving our definition of success. What this means is that, even though difficulties arise, we are the ones who define ourselves as being optimistic or pessimistic, victims or victors, loving or distant, in control or out of control, fearful or confident, uncertain or self-assured.

Nobody else can be held accountable for these choices. If we're not getting what we think we want from life, maybe we need to look back at the way we have defined ourselves. We become the managers of our eternal destiny based on the definitions that we create.

We've spent a lifetime establishing and developing patterns, and we tend to define ourselves by these patterns. Although it seems that these patterns could inspire personal growth because of their imperfections, they actually retard growth as long as they persist. Because of these dynamics, it's essential that we redefine ourselves by the insight we have developed from our mistakes, not by the mistakes themselves.

In life, we find purpose, reason, and wisdom. Nothing is wasted— not even our most difficult and painful experiences. So expect to succeed. Live life by design, not by accident.

Today is not a drill, and this moment is not a dress rehearsal. We have prepared our entire lives for this performance. We don't want to miss it because of hesitation, and we don't want to blow it because of fear. Since life has probably not been completely accommodating in the past, maybe we need to commit ourselves to a new belief system for the future. As we dare to develop a new way of looking at ourselves, we'll discover that destiny is not a matter of chance, but rather a matter of choice.

We can't afford to wobble with uncertainty. It hurts too much. We can't afford not to go first-class; there is no good reason to settle for less. Ultimately, we are the determining factor in the equation. We are completely successful in achieving our definition of happiness.

SOONER OR LATER

Sooner or later, the time comes in your life when you take an honest, realistic look at yourself. You cast aside all the excuses and defenses that have made growth and development so difficult, and you ask yourself the gateway questions: Who am I? What do I stand for? What are the guiding principles in my life?

Sooner or later, things begin to change, but until they do, the old familiar problems continue to rear their ugly heads. Insight never quite catches up with you, understanding seems to pass you by, wisdom remains just beyond your reach, and you find yourself asking the question, "How did all this happen?"

Sooner or later, when the time is right and you get sick and tired of being sick and tired, new doors and pathways begin to open that you did not previously recognize, and you realize that you're finally on a positive track. But by itself, this realization is not enough. As Will Rogers put it, "Even if you're on the right track, you'll get run over if you just sit there."[1] In other words, once you find the right course, you must actively pursue it in a positive way. Such an effort can be difficult, but it is not so difficult once you realize you're in a position to manage your eternal destiny!

Sooner or later, you understand that self-control is strength and that it all begins with holding yourself accountable to eternal principles. You find that thinking right is mastery, and it results from learning— not only from your own mistakes but also from the mistakes of others. As you rise to a higher plane, it becomes increasingly clear that calmness is power. Leonardo da Vinci has written, "He who truly knows has no reason to shout."[2]

Sooner or later, you find that managing your own destiny is a complicated process of blending old values with new ideas and of turning dreams into reality. Sometimes this transition can be a little rough. So remember, success in life is a lifelong process and not the result of any single victory or failure.

Sooner or later, you realize that if you're not actively trying to become the person you want to be, then you are becoming the person you don't want to be. Based on the kind of principles you apply, either correct or incorrect, there is a natural law that dictates you will get exactly what you deserve in this world. That may sound harsh, but it's just the result of natural laws. We draw to ourselves what we believe, either positive or negative. And we radiate to others what we are, either authentic or disingenuous.

Sooner or later, you begin to understand that education is not intelligence, that wealth is not happiness, and that physical intimacy is not love. You find that happiness is found somewhere in between having too much and having too little and that happiness is not a goal, but a by-product.

Sooner or later, you find that the greatest disservice you can do for yourself is to limit your own expectations. By becoming too complacent with things as they are or by rejecting things as they might be, by fearing the unknown or by always playing it safe, you become your own worst enemy.

Sooner or later, you realize that ships were made for more than being anchored safely in the harbor. Success in life comes through striving and achieving, not through passively accepting whatever comes your way, and you finally realize that to accept less than what you're capable of achieving is, in part, to die.

Sooner or later, as your insight increases and your understanding becomes more complete, it will result in pure wisdom. Your perception begins to change, you experience, you learn, and you seek new paths. When the time is right, you go where there are no paths and leave a trail for others to follow. After all is said and done, maybe that's what life is all about anyway.

NOTES

1.   Will Rogers, "Spoken Words," accessed December 12, 2011, http://www.anand.to/quotes/search.php?search=will+rogers.

2.   Leonardo da Vinci, "Thought of the Day Archive," accessed December 12, 2011, http://www.refdesk.com/apr04td.html.

CHAPTER 10

A CHANGE OF HEART

WHEN OUR DAUGHTER WAS SEVENTEEN YEARS OLD, she played the part of Belle in her high school musical production of *Beauty and the Beast*. This particular version of the tale begins with an old beggar woman arriving at the castle of a French prince. The elderly woman asks for shelter from the cold and in return, offers the young prince a beautiful, red rose. Repulsed by her appearance, he refuses to assist her. The woman warns him not to be deceived by outward appearances. The prince still decides to turn her away. She then throws off her disguise, revealing that she is a beautiful enchantress. The prince immediately begins to apologize, but she has already witnessed his unkindness. She transforms him into a hideous creature that reflects the selfishness inside of him. Additionally, the entire castle is changed into a dark, forbidding place so he will learn not to judge others so harshly. The only way for him to break the curse is to learn to love and accept others' love in return before the last petal of the enchantress's rose withers and falls from the stem. If he chooses not to do this, he will be doomed to remain a beast forever. As the years pass, the beast lives in his castle, wallowing in sadness and despair, convinced that he will never change.

Fortunately, the beast eventually meets a beautiful young woman named Belle. Over time, she helps him to see the goodness inside himself and in others. Through her kindness and love, the curse is broken, and he becomes a new man. He experiences a change of heart, which enables him to show sincere love, tenderness, and patience. He leaves behind the dark despair of his former self and chooses to pursue a life filled with happiness, joy, and peace. His outward actions match the goodness inside of him.

We too must work to experience a similar transformation. That is, we need to make a concerted effort to overcome selfishness and pride and replace them with love and humility.

The scriptures are filled with examples of how God's people are sometimes compelled to be humble. We read about natural disasters such as great earthquakes, whirlwinds, and floods that caused the proud and powerful to be brought down and humbled. Famine, drought, pestilence, and war are also mentioned in the scriptures and were a part of the process of helping those afflicted by these conditions to become humble.

On a more personal level, I've found the experiences we encounter every day serve to humble us and can help turn our hearts to God. Wayward children, prolonged illness, financial hardships, mental illness, abuse, or personal weaknesses may help us to recognize our dependence on God and our own nothingness without his divine support.

Jesus Christ has given us a model for developing humility. His disciples approached him and inquired, "Who is the greatest in the kingdom of heaven?" He responded by placing a little child in their midst and stating, "Whosoever therefore shall humble himself as this little child, the same is greatest in the kingdom of heaven" (Matthew 18:1, 4). We know the process of becoming like a child takes time—a lifetime and possibly beyond. Therefore, we must exercise faith and patience along the way.

When we are humble, we strive to forgive those who have offended us and let go of grudges. When humble, we show our love for God by losing ourselves in his service and letting go of worldly things.

When I think of holding on to worldly things, I'm reminded of a story about monkey traps. In Malaysia the natives have a unique, effective way to capture monkeys. They lop the top off a coconut, remove the meat, and leave a hole in the top of the coconut large enough for the monkey to put his paw in. Then they anchor the coconut to the ground and put some peanuts in it. When the hunters leave, the monkeys, smelling those delicious peanuts, approach the coconuts, see the peanuts inside, and reach in to remove the nuts—but find that the hole is too small for their doubled-up fists. The natives return with gunnysacks and pick up the monkeys. The monkeys claw, bite, and scream, but they will not drop the peanuts to save their lives.[1]

Are we sometimes like the monkey caught in the trap, where the things that matter most in life are at the mercy of those things that matter least? With so many worldly enticements, do we fiercely hold on to those things of an ephemeral nature at the expense of those things of eternal value? Do we sometimes even find ourselves hanging on to unhealthy patterns of behavior because we simply don't know what else to do?

For most of my life, I've struggled to let go of false pride. Nevertheless, what appeared to serve as a source of strength during my teenage years became a stumbling block as an adult. My skills as an athlete, appearance, and even my religious beliefs made me feel I was better than others. Such thoughts and feelings were a feeble attempt to fill the void I felt inside and establish a sense of my own worth.

I've since learned that false pride and its companion, shame, cause us to feel superior or inferior to others. Both are unhealthy responses. They contribute to the development of a distorted sense of who we really are. That is why Jesus has invited us to overcome pride and shame by working to eliminate feelings of superiority and inferiority, putting our trust in God and not in superficial or temporal things.

Most of us, if we are honest with ourselves, will find we may have the tendency to place too much emphasis on making external changes, cheap substitutes if you will, for the internal changes required to bring real happiness. This is a natural response, which is not good or bad but is part of the process of learning to overcome false pride. It may be material possessions, educational and career achievements, or our physical appearance. These are only a few examples of the many ways we may attempt to gratify our pride and vain ambitions. Eventually, we must learn to put our trust in God and not in those things that temporarily fill our emotional and spiritual void providing us with only a pseudo sense of our true worth.

I believe false pride serves as an artificial substitute for emotional wellness. That is why good emotional health is so important. It provides the foundation for spiritual growth that allows one to eventually experience a change of heart.

I now more fully understand that real happiness comes only through serving God and putting him first. It comes as we humble ourselves and seek his guidance in all we do.

At times we may feel a bit discouraged when we consider the spiritual gap between where we are now and where we would like to be. We can take comfort in recognizing that God knows each of us individually, he understands our needs and desires perfectly and is eager to bless us fully. As we strive to keep God's commandments and humbly follow Christ, he will patiently and lovingly help us overcome false pride, shame, and other personal challenges, and provide us with experiences that will help soften our hearts and strengthen our love for others.

CLINICAL INSIGHTS

BUT IF NOT . . .

We hope we will be able to escape most of the major discomforts in life, but if not, we'll eventually discover that the benefits of life will far exceed the discomforts.

We hope we will be protected from the injustices in life, but if not, we'll learn to manage them, and we'll grow stronger because of them. Nothing is wasted.

We hope we will be appreciated for who we are, but if not, we'll learn to accept life for what it is, and we'll continue to make our contributions anyway.

We hope we will be loved as we want to be loved, but if not, we'll learn that as we work on ourselves, others will eventually be drawn to us. Like interlocking pieces of a puzzle, our lives are interrelated. We are all a part of the whole.

We hope our bodies and minds will remain whole and healthy, but if not, the significance of life will continue to expand in spite of our imperfections. Life has purpose, and we are part of something greater.

We hope we will be respected for our knowledge, our experience, and our abilities, but if not, we'll learn that it's possible to be okay without the constant validation and approval of others.

We hope our relationships with others will be healthy and satisfying, but if not, we'll learn that we can alter imperfect patterns and that as we do less of what doesn't work and more of what does, the world will change—and so will we.

We hope we will develop a comfortable level of certainty with our future, but if not, eventually we'll discover that we can live well, even with a certain amount of uncertainty.

We hope we will discover how all the pieces of life fit together, but if not, the experiences of life will continue to shape our destiny, and we will learn to manage the incompleteness.

We hope we will discover the benefits of living life by design, but if not, the consequences of our old choices will force us to dream new dreams. As a result, we'll discover new worlds.

THE BASICS

We are unique. As we discover who we really are, we begin to accept that we are the way we are, that life is the way it is, and that it has real purpose. We each have a variety of gifts, characteristics, weaknesses, and inabilities that separate us from all others, and they literally prepare us to accomplish certain things in life. Nothing is wasted. So we overcome what we can, accept what we can't, and do what we can in spite of what we can't. In this manner, we will touch the lives of those around us in ways that only we can.

We have infinite worth. Our greatest strength lies in our self-worth. We didn't come in to this world to get self-worth; we brought it with us. It was a gift. It was part of the package we were given. It never goes away, and it has nothing to do with our performance. Our job is not to develop our self-worth but rather to discover it. We can then use that knowledge to rise above our previous selves.

We are part of something greater. We're not alone in this world. Our existence has a divine purpose, and we are here for a reason. The choices we make, the principles we use, and the roles we play are all part of a life that is orchestrated for our benefit and development. With this in mind, we need to be consistently shifting our focus from a temporal perspective to an eternal one.

We have a significance that affects all areas of life. Our significance refers to our ability to make a difference in life. It's what we do with our self-worth that affects us socially, emotionally, physically, spiritually, and financially. Our significance never goes away, but when we feel we have no significance, it affects the way we interpret our challenges and results in potential impairment in all areas of life.

We are responsible for our choices. There is a cause-and-effect relationship between the choices we make and the changes that occur in life. As we make new choices, changes occur automatically. Ultimately, we are responsible for these choices—no one else is. As these principles become more deeply embedded in our lives, a natural change occurs, and personal responsibility is converted into personal accountability. When this occurs, we are able to see the world from a different point of view, and we are never, ever the same.

We are capable. When we do our part, we will develop capabilities and life-management skills as we need them. As time passes, we will progress and attract to ourselves those things on which we focus. What distresses us, overwhelms us, or strengthens us invariably becomes integrated into who we are. We are a work in progress. We're not done yet.

If we can visualize it, we can achieve it. As we rise to a higher level of functioning, a change must take place—not only in our behavior but also in our thinking. If we follow old patterns, we will maintain our old, limited perception. So make the decision to engage the magic that exists in powerful imagery. Don't settle for mediocrity. When we can visualize and imagine something, it materializes and creates an energy that manifests itself in our minds. This imagery is a force that can be used to transform the ordinary into the extraordinary, the common into the unique. It unifies the power of mind, body, and spirit as it converts the "storms of conflict" into the "river of experience" and the "waves of emotion" into the "peace of serenity."

Perspective is everything. Don't let the apparent imperfections in life fool you. Life is not a disease. There is no cure for it. Natural laws dictate that where there is pain, there will eventually be growth. Where there is chaos, organization will follow. Where there is limitation or restriction, freedom will be achieved. In this manner, the cycles of life repeat themselves as they follow the natural laws of life. As you take charge of these cycles, you'll find that you can manage all of them.

Commit yourself to being surprised. Life is full of color, beauty, and opportunities, but you must believe it before you will be able to see it. So don't take life for granted, don't put yourself on autopilot, and don't have near-life experiences! Dare to do mighty things. No one benefits when you choose not to do so. You can break self-defeating patterns and reprogram incorrect belief systems. Whether you think you can or you can't, you're right!

Commit yourself to life. We can find purpose, reason, and wisdom in life. We're often unable to fully appreciate life because of our limited perspective. In an attempt to feel good, we often take the path of least resistance, and we end up sabotaging our happiness. Yes, feeling good is important, but feeling good is not enough. It doesn't last. When we finally reach the point in life where our vision becomes clearer and we commit ourselves to the higher road, we begin to realize that it's possible to feel better than just good. Only then will we find a freedom and a peace of mind that will follow us for the rest of our lives.

AT TIMES

At times, it appears that we all get lost. We lose our direction, we lose our motivation, and nothing seems to make any sense. When this occurs, it's often because we feel confusion in one or more of the following areas:

1. What is the purpose of our existence?

2. What is the role we have chosen to play in life?

3. What kind of legacy are we creating?

When we get lost, it simply means we have temporarily forgotten the answers to these questions. It is through the process of finding these answers that we find ourselves once again.

We have lessons to learn, tears to shed, people to love, and beauty to share. We can gain wisdom from experiencing the exhilaration and freedom of the light-filled times in our lives, and we can gain emotional depth from tolerating the intolerability of darkness. Life is full of these lessons. Life is never wasted.

Sometimes the apparent futility of learning these lessons makes us believe that we should give up and that it's a waste of time to keep trying because things are already as good as they can be. It's easy to get lost in this kind of thinking. In reality, we are "becoming," and we only become by beginning again and again.

If we ever believe that it's too late to begin again, we rob ourselves of what we might have become. We need to remember that no one gets it right the first time! We must pay a price to gain insight. This process of becoming requires much more than just concern, more than commitment, and more than determination. It requires a revolution! Because the breadth and depth of our patterns of behavior often span generations, it may take forever to become what we want to be. As a result, nothing short of a revolution will have the power to redirect our lives.

One of the fundamental elements in this revolutionary process, and the standard by which all things are clarified, is self-mastery. The best of us and the worst of us. We develop self-mastery when we recognize that while both of these possibilities exist, we consistently make the choices that take us on the higher road.

Self-mastery allows us to listen to and evaluate what's going on in the world around us and then to integrate the wisdom that we've been prepared to accept. Self-mastery also allows us to be aware of what's going on inside of us, to envision what our potential is, and to grow into who we are capable of becoming. When viewed from this perspective, the development of self-mastery becomes one of the essential defining moments in life.

NOTES

1. "The Monkey Trap," accessed December 12, 2011, http://truth-spring.info/2008/01/19/themonkey-trap.

CHAPTER 11

WHAT EXPERIENCE CAN TEACH US

BY JOHN WATERBURY

I'M A SMALL-TOWN COUNTRY BOY FROM SOUTHERN ILLI-nois. I've had my share of challenges, but they have probably been no more or less than what most others experience. Throughout my life, I've been involved in a seemingly insignificant array of positive events that have come and gone without much attention. Some of those events made an impression on me, but most did not. Fortunately, I see things differently now. Now I strive to be alert to those positive experiences, which I consider to be God's tender mercies. I try not to let them slip by as I did before.

I believe that, when this life is over, everyone is going to meet God. He is going to ask us to account for what we did with what we were given. If I didn't know what I know now, my report would be somewhat lacking in color and vibrancy.

"Well, John," he would say. "It's time. Give me an accounting of your life."

I would respond, "You're probably aware that I got the short end of the straw on earth. Everyone around me had been given so much more. The person next door was rich, and the person across the street was very intelligent. It just wasn't fair. Everyone was blessed more than

I was. How could you expect anything of significance from me since I was given so little?"

"No," he would say. "You weren't given everything, but you were given what you needed to complete your assignment and fulfill your purpose in life. Now tell me, what did you do with what you were given?"

"Well, since I wasn't given much, I tried to make do with what I had. I experienced a difficult childhood, and life wasn't always fair to me, but, despite overwhelming odds, I hung in there somehow. I remained a good Christian, but because I was given so little, I was unable to make much of a contribution. I obtained a good education, but I had to move all over the country just to find employment. I was married and raised a family, but it was clear to everyone that I was far from being a perfect husband and father. That's my report, unfortunately."

He would then say in a soft, loving voice, "Do you believe that you were an accident and that no forethought went into your assignment in life? Do you think that I would let you wander aimlessly through life with no purpose in mind?"

"Well, the thought had crossed my mind," I would reply.

He would then say, "Do you remember back in 1967, when you were visiting with your neighbor, Mrs. Babb? Do you remember what you said to her?"

"No."

"You didn't know it, but what you said was just what she needed to hear," he would say. "Do you remember riding the bus in Chicago and talking to a woman about a problem she was having with her son?"

"No."

"Well, what you told her was just what she needed to know at the time. It brought peace and hope to her mind. Do you remember your interview with a teenager in Owensboro, Kentucky, or the guy who responded to your radio talk show in Austin, Texas?"

"No."

He would then say, "You were right where you were supposed to be and doing exactly what you were supposed to be doing, according to the important life assignment you had been given. There were hundreds of other times like these. You didn't think that they were all just coincidences did you?"

I'm convinced there are numerous examples in each of our lives where small miracles are manifested. Sometimes we recognize them, but for the most part we go on about our lives, oblivious to their significance and meaning. Maybe that's the way it's supposed to be. The story included below is an example of what I mean.

I had been working nights in the Chicago area with the Salvation Army, running individual and group sessions with the transient population. It was fascinating work. Instead of trying to teach life-management skills, communication skills, and family problem-resolution skills, the main goals were to simply help the clients stay alive.

They came and they went—nameless faces from nameless places. They hopped freight trains and traveled to where the weather and the food were better than what they had. Few had any roots, and even fewer had any aspirations. Those had been given up long ago, somewhere along their life's journey. Some had families. Some didn't. Some died ,and others survived the harsh conditions. That was life on the streets.

I'd been there for two years when I received a letter from a man who had lived on the streets. No one had ever heard of anything like that happening before. No one recognized the name of the man who sent it. He wrote:

> Dear John,
>
> I just had to take the time to write you. About two years ago I was there at the Salvation Army, and what you said to me turned my life around. I'm out here in California now. I've been working steady for quite a while, and I just got married to a woman with two kids. I've never been happier and life has never been better. I just thought you'd like to know.

To this day, I can't remember the man's name or face. No one at the Salvation Army could remember him either. But even worse, I can't remember the magic words I told him. He must have only been there long enough to get a bed and a few meals and then he moved on. But at least once our paths crossed, something good happened. Apparently, I was right where I was supposed to be and doing what I needed to be doing. It reaffirmed the fact that God's plan is perfect, and as we become more aware of his influence in our lives, we begin to more clearly and regularly recognize his influence.

A few months later, another man came up to me on the street with a big smile on his face. He said, "John Waterbury, it's great to see you again! Remember last year when I was broke and you helped me out and I said I'd never forget you?"

"Yes, I remember," I enthusiastically replied, once again expecting some small miracle to occur because of my dedicated service at the Salvation Army.

"Well," he said, as he stuck his hand out, "I'm broke again!" I guess you can't win them all, but you can win some of them.

CLINICAL INSIGHTS

PAIN PRECEDES CHANGE

One small act of kindness can help change another person's life. All of us are affected by these dynamics. Our lives and the lives of those around us seem to be coordinated in a manner that is hard for us to understand. We can't ignore the fact that each life touches many others.

A good example of this is the life of Helen Keller. Most people have heard the story of how she rose above the challenges of being deaf and blind and how she touched the lives of millions of others with disabilities. What is often overlooked are the people who were prepared to be brought into her life to assist her, guide her, and love her enough to allow her to accomplish her purpose in life.

As the various stories go, a nurse met a little, partially blind orphan girl named Ann Sullivan. That nurse recognized the potential that "Little Annie" possessed, and it was through her efforts that Annie was nurtured and encouraged to be able to grow and develop as an independent, educated young woman. This growth prepared Anne Sullivan to be brought into the life of Helen Keller as her teacher. She was able to touch Helen Keller's life in ways that only she could.

We are each prepared to influence those around us. Yet we tend to overlook the significant influence we have in others' lives, or the influence they have in ours, when we focus on our inabilities and limitations. We seldom clearly understand what we accomplish in this world, the directions we take, and how we impact the lives of others. One thing is certain—as long as we are looking for the guidance and direction Jesus Christ provides us, we will be led along a path that will bless the lives of others as well as our own.

Let me illustrate this point with a personal story. A number of years ago, my wife and I were living in Knoxville, Tennessee. We had one five-year-old daughter, and after several miscarriages, it seemed we were not going to be able to have any more children. I was fine with this, but my wife was frustrated. We both eventually agreed to consider the possibility of adoption. After searching for several months, we decided to consider adopting a child from South America, and we made contacts with the appropriate agency. One of the requirements was having a family history completed by the local family services agency, so we made an appointment.

While we were sitting in the social worker's office at the agency, she received a phone call from a couple who had adopted three children ten months earlier. The couple had a ten-year-old boy when they started the paperwork, but they had been unable to have any more children. The adoption went as planned. They were given the three children, and, immediately, the woman became pregnant. Nine months later she delivered a healthy baby, and, soon after, became pregnant again. There they were with almost three biological children and three adopted children. Apparently, that was too much for them, and—through an interesting series of events—the three adopted children were brought into our lives. To us, it was nothing short of a miracle.

THE PERFECT PURPOSE OF PAIN

Let's assume that this is a perfect world, or rather, a perfectly imperfect world in which everything is designed to fall apart. Everywhere we look, we see pain. Since there is so much pain in this perfect world, it only makes sense that pain must be an essential part of our experience. It's not our nemesis, as some would have us believe, but rather it's one of the greatest motivating forces in life. The ancient philosopher Euripides said, "There is in the worst of fortune the best chances for a happy change."[1]

Pain has a significance that few of us understand. When viewed with the big picture in mind, it appears that pain influences every aspect of life. Therefore, instead of trying to avoid the pain and problems, maybe we should try to face them and embrace them. It's only when we do so that we are able to derive their full benefits.

The greatest strengths and insights that we develop are the direct result of our personal battles. Such battles include battles with challenges that we thought were insurmountable, battles with overwhelming obstacles, and battles with problems that we thought would never resolve. It's the presence of pain that forces us to fight these battles, and it's pain that forces us to learn the lessons that only these battles can teach.

Eventually, we learn that we attract to ourselves what we focus on, that we are drawn toward what we think we are, and that we limit ourselves to what we think we deserve. These principles form the foundation upon which we must build a life. Pain forces us to continually redefine ourselves as we take charge of this process.

Even though we may try to maintain our old self-defeating thoughts and behaviors, the pain that results encourages us to choose a higher level of functioning. Pain teaches that there is no end to our development because we are constantly changing and progressing.

Pain allows for discontent, serving to deepen our awareness of our old limits, and gives us the incentive to grow beyond them. Pain allows for discouragement that forces us to draw upon a power greater than ourselves. We deny the need to change until the pain becomes unbearable. Only then do we become willing to make new choices.

Pain forces us to light a candle in the darkness, and then it teaches us that a candle loses nothing by lighting other candles—or in other words, that we lose nothing by helping others and accepting help. Pain forces us to discover our natural gifts and abilities. Pain reinforces the fact that we need to combine a belief in ourselves with a desire to put that belief into action. Pain forces us to realize that no one is capable of doing for us what we have to do for ourselves. Pain forces us to carve out a niche in life, or a pattern that enables us to manage life. That pattern is then replicated throughout the rest of our lives. Pain forces us to develop a pain-management philosophy that empowers us to rise to previously unexpected levels of achievement.

Pain makes it possible to move from distraction to discernment, from chaos to clarity, and from distress to design. Pain gives us power—power to achieve, power to grow, power to become. Pain prepares us to accept transformations to the higher roads in life.

NOTES

1. Euripedes, accessed January 2, 2012, http://en.wikiquote.org/wiki/Euripides.

CHAPTER 12

DO THE RIGHT THING
FOR THE RIGHT REASON

AS I'VE REFLECTED ON THE NEED TO DO THE RIGHT thing for the right reason and how it relates to spiritual growth, I've been reminded of those times when my immediate family and I have done the right thing for the wrong reason. For example, several years ago as we prepared for bed, we knelt down together for prayer. Knowing that my wife had said prayer that morning, I asked our oldest son to say the prayer. He reminded us that he had said it the night before, so I then asked our daughter. She said she was too tired. Finally, I asked our four-year-old son, Landon. He also claimed he was too tired to say the prayer. Annoyed by their responses, I reluctantly announced I would say it. At that point Landon blurted out, "Okay, okay, I'll say it. At least that way I know it will be short!"

Doing the right thing for the right reason can be an ongoing challenge. It certainly has been for me. For most of my life, I've tried hard to do all that was expected of me. However, my motivation wasn't always my love for God. I was under the mistaken impression that if I did all of the right things, as I perceived them, somehow the pain from my childhood would be removed, my immediate family would be spared having to suffer as I did, and God would love me more.

I became obsessive about my own and others' behaviors in an attempt to control the outcomes. I wanted my family life to be different from what I experienced as a child. I foolishly expected perfection from my wife and children in hopes that we wouldn't have to endure similar hardships.

I experienced the painful prison of perfectionism. The prison foundation was built from creating standards that were beyond the reach and reason of myself and others and were the direct result of childhood experiences. The prison included bricks of depression from when I experienced failure and disappointment; stones of preoccupation from my fear of failure and disapproval that depleted my emotional and physical energy; bars from viewing mistakes as evidence of unworthiness; and locks from becoming overly defensive whenever I was criticized.

Through the power of the atonement and with the support of a loving wife, I eventually figured out how to do the right things for the right reasons. Developing childlike love and patience was the key that helped unlock the prison doors. I was released from the prison of perfectionism and learned to enjoy the process, as well as the outcome. I discovered how to bounce back from failure and disappointment quickly and with energy and how to keep normal anxiety and fear of failure and disapproval within bounds, using them to be energized not enervated. I also began to view mistakes as opportunities for growth and learning and reacted more positively to helpful criticism. I gradually became less obsessed with being the perfect husband and parent and more aware of the need to show love, patience, and understanding. Through my life experiences, I've learned simply doing the right things is not enough. We must also do them for the right reasons—out of love for God, for others, and for ourselves.

As a child, I had learned from my father that there are two sets of behavioral expectations—one for how you behave in public and the other for how you behave in the privacy of your home. After marrying and having a family of my own, I found my public and private behaviors were also inconsistent. I was short-tempered with my wife and our children, and I struggled to show the love and patience they desperately needed and deserved. Nevertheless, I was diligent in fulfilling my church and professional obligations with patience. Laurie and our children also discovered I behaved differently outside the home. Fortunately, they were patient and forgiving as I struggled to become a better husband and father.

Over the years, I mistakenly believed I was justified in harshly judging my father's intentions and actions because of the way he treated us. It has only been during the last few years that I began to better understand the scripture found in Matthew 7:1–5:

> Judge not, that ye be not judged. For with what judgment ye judge, ye shall be judged: and with what measure ye mete, it shall be measured to you again. And why beholdest thou the mote that is in they brother's eye, but considerest not the beam that is in thine own eye? Or how will thou say to thy brother, Let me pull out the mote out of thine eye; and, behold, a beam is in thine own eye? Thou hypocrite, first cast out the beam out of thine own eye; and then shalt thou see clearly to cast out the mote out of thy brother's eye.

It has been said you can't judge someone and also love them. I would add that you can't judge someone and also love yourself. Unrighteous judgment of my father and others prevented me from clearly seeing my many shortcomings. It adversely impacted my ability to heal emotionally, to grow spiritually, and to love God, others, and myself.

The Apostle Paul was buffeted with a personal challenge he referred to as a "thorn in the flesh" (2 Corinthians 12:7). He pleaded with God that it might be removed. He responded by saying, "My grace is sufficient for thee: for my strength is made perfect in weakness. Most gladly therefore will I rather glory in my infirmities, that the power of Christ may rest upon me . . . for when I am weak, then am I strong" (2 Corinthians 12:9–10).

Humility, or the recognition that we need God's help to manage our weaknesses, magnify our strengths, and overcome our sins, is essential for spiritual growth. This growth process also necessitates that we have a healthy understanding of the difference between sin and weakness. They are not the same. Sin is any deliberate disobedience to the known will of God[1] while weakness, in this context, refers to inherent abilities, conditions, and traits that are a part of being mortal (for example, physical limitations, mental illness, learning and cognitive disabilities, sensory impairments, and so on). We do not choose them. Nevertheless, humility can help us to learn and grow from our weaknesses and sins rather than be destroyed by them. In life, spiritual growth and doing the right things for the right reasons are built on a strong foundation of humility.

Regular, sincere prayer helps us to be humble and increases our sensitivity to those areas of our life we may need to change. Prayer can also help us to forgive others. Our prayers may include a petition for humility and charity.

As we combine prayer with scripture study, we are more easily directed by God, especially as we continue to respond to his guidance. Daily scripture study helps us to enjoy daily personal inspiration.

Humility, sincere prayer, and scripture study guide us to do those things that are right and good, and they help us become doers of the word and not hearers only. We develop increased integrity and naturally choose to do the right things for the right reasons. We enjoy greater inner peace and serenity. The guilt, shame, and anxiety that come from perfectionism and other personal challenges begin to disappear.

This is what it's all about—doing what God would have us do and striving to be like Jesus. That is how we are able to do the right thing for the right reason. As we do, we naturally begin to align what we know and do with what we earnestly desire to be.

CLINICAL INSIGHTS

CLARITY

Let's face it—we're off course! Everyone is to some degree. We don't need to worry about being off course as long as we're committed to making a series of minor course corrections. That's the key!

Some time ago, Dr. David Donaldson, a pediatric endocrinologist, shared a thought-provoking concept with me: "That which can be measured can be managed." While his statement referred to the treatment of childhood diabetes, it also has a direct application to the field of psychotherapy. That which can be measured, or defined, can be understood. And that which can be understood can be managed.

The problem is that many people who experience emotional distress don't understand what caused them to be off course in the first place. If they are unable to accurately define those disabling factors, then they tend to repeat the self-defeating patterns until their patterns control them. The key is increased understanding, and understanding results in clarity. Once we are able to see ourselves and our problems clearly, we have developed clarity.

Clarity shows that our greatest strength lies not in the absence of vulnerability but in the decision to rise above its immobilizing effects.

Clarity helps us understand that since there are no victims without volunteers, the victims can become victors.

Clarity reveals that happiness, peace of mind, and even sanity itself cannot be measured by how far we have to go, but by how far we have come.

Clarity teaches that the value we place upon ourselves determines the quality of the people we allow into our lives. We only attract people we feel worthy of, and we never let ourselves have more love than we think we deserve.

Clarity emphasizes that we only grow stronger, increase our self-esteem, and improve our self-confidence when we take risks, make new choices, and move outside of old comfort zones.

Clarity helps us recognize that there is often purpose in confusion and design in imperfections. When managed effectively, confusion and imperfections become blessings in disguise.

Clarity helps us to redefine the past, create a new future, and overcome and outgrow the old restrictive patterns that were previously taken for granted and thought to be normal.

Clarity unifies our mind, body, and spirit.

Clarity strengthens not only our own lives, but the lives of everyone we come in contact with.

Clarity emphasizes that there is no need to fear the process of examining, participating, and becoming one with life.

Clarity occurs when we realize that life is what is, not what was and not what might have been.

Clarity helps us understand that what we choose to believe about ourselves is what becomes real and that while our history may have been a matter of chance, our destiny is a matter of choice.

Clarity shows that we can use the pain and imperfections in life as excuses or as incentives to adapt and change for the better.

Clarity helps us to not confuse who we really are with what we do now or what we have done.

Clarity reveals that we are the ones who determine the path we follow. When we decide to change our course, it's clarity that helps us realize that it's not the world that has changed.

Clarity occurs when we finally realize that the greatest opportunities seldom come in the manner we would have chosen.

Clarity teaches that when we choose not to grow beyond what we were, we will fail to become what we might have been.

Clarity makes it possible to synergize, to achieve, to grow, and to become. It reminds us that we are the only one who can take charge of that process.

Clarity helps us realize that painful life problems are like fertilizer. They don't smell very good, but in their wake they leave growth, depth, and color that could have been achieved in no other way in their wake.

Clarity encourages us to make a difference—to touch a life and create a legacy.

PERSPECTIVE IS EVERYTHING

Our view of the world is constantly changing, and our perspective continues to expand as we learn to see the world more accurately. Sometimes as this process unfolds, we tend to focus on the pain, and we overlook the personal development that results from coping with the pain.

In reality, as we learn to adapt to ever-changing conditions, we develop flexibility. As we learn to accept the inevitable, we develop resilience. As we consistently face the unavoidable, we develop confidence. As we conform to higher expectations, we develop discipline, and as we put the pieces of life's puzzle together, the picture of who we really are becomes clearer.

It all boils down to this: we can complain about the ruts in the road, or we can accept that the ruts are the road! Because of these ruts, we learn lessons that alter our perspective in ways that almost defy understanding. There are three main principles that seem to form the foundation for this process. They include the following:

1. We can only achieve personal freedom and discover the beauty that surrounds us when we are secure enough to relax and appreciate life.

2. We can only achieve that level of security when we prepare for life and develop the kind of confidence that leads to peace of mind.

3. Peace of mind only materializes when we realize that we will always be able to manage any of the challenges and problems we face, either by ourselves or with the help of others.

With this foundation in place, we begin to understand that the impossible is not impossible—there is always a solution. We discover that seldom is any loss irreplaceable, for almost everything can be replaced, and the intolerable doesn't have to remain intolerable, for we can always learn to adjust. We are the ones who define the circumstances of our lives.

Unfortunately, unhappiness and fear often complicate the way we create these definitions. Unhappiness occurs when we believe that the mistakes of the past cannot be rectified and that our old self-defeating behaviors and unhealthy thinking patterns are unalterable. Fear makes us believe the problems of life are bigger than our abilities to resolve them. But they're not!

Everything can be altered, rebuilt, or replaced, and new knowledge can result in new skills that can overcome any problem. That is why it's so important to remember that problems are always purposeful. Some are meant to be solved, some are meant to change our course, and some are meant to be accepted and endured. Problems literally reshape, refine, and redesign who we are and what we can be. They result in depth and clarity that can be achieved in no other way. Problems remind us that perspective is everything.

THE LIMITS OF OUR REALITY

When we repeatedly feel as if our lives have become overwhelming, it's almost certain that our perception has become imperfect. For it is not the world that controls who we are or how we react or which course we take in life. Through the experiences we have and the resulting choices we make, we are the ones who determine the role we play in the theater of life. Despite the successes and failures of the past, we are the ones who determine how we will manage the challenges of our world today. We are the ones who define both our reality and ourselves. Once we understand this great responsibility, all things become possible.

We can always choose what attitude we will have in the face of any circumstances. Specifically, we are not our past, although we are touched by it. We are not our fear, although we are drawn to it. We are not our pain, although we develop because of it. The choices we make and the attitudes we develop are constantly changing as we move from one transitional phase to another.

There's no end to this process. This means that, sooner or later, what we have now is going to change. Those who are failing will find success. Those who are overwhelmed with pain will find relief. Those who are lost will find the path.

No one will escape these essential emotional and spiritual dynamics. The result will be a continuing process of redefining ourselves and of growing beyond ourselves. In this manner, we alter the limits of our reality.

There are many things in life that seem impossible, and some of them actually are. When something is truly impossible, another option invariably becomes inevitable. As a result, when our movement in any given direction becomes impossible, it becomes inevitable that other possibilities will be discovered. The goal is to develop a philosophy of life that enables us to actually believe that the impossible always leads to the inevitability of new possibilities. This is why our attitude is so important.

Without patience and faith, it would be easy to become overwhelmed. If we are overwhelmed now, it's easy to believe we will always feel that way—but we won't.

Hence, when you're in the midst of a struggle, remind yourself that life exposes us to sensations and powerful emotions that have the capacity to build or to destroy. Based on the choices we consistently make, one or the other will result. We are the ones who define the limits of our reality.

NOTES

1.   Free Dictionary, accessed June 26, 2012, http://www.thefreedictionary.com/Sin.

CHAPTER 13

KNOWING, DOING, AND BEING

I'VE REACHED THE POINT IN LIFE WHERE I NOW REALIZE that merely knowing and doing are insufficient for helping us to become more like the Savior. I've learned we can know what is right and do what appears to be right but still miss the mark. Real peace, joy, and happiness in life require that we strive to align what we know and do with what we earnestly desire to be. The difference is that we may sincerely believe we are doing right things but not experiencing the change in our hearts described in the scriptures.

Such a change causes us to be more authentic in our relationships with God and others and eliminate hypocrisy from our lives. Jesus Christ repeatedly illustrated the differences between the pure in heart and those who pretended to be. For example, he frequently admonished, "And when thou prayest thou shalt not do as the hypocrites, for they love to pray, standing in the synagogues and in the corners of the streets, that they may be seen of men. Verily I say unto you, They have their reward" (Matthew 6:5).

We recognize that doing is an essential part of Christ's teachings. However, doing must be combined with being. That is, both our actions and our natures must be patterned after Christ's. This involves more than merely going through the motions, like we sometimes have the tendency to do, or pretending to be something we are not. The Greek word for *pretender* means "play actor, or one who feigns, represents dramatically, or exaggerates a part." As our natures change, so do the motivations behind our actions. We become motivated to serve God for the right reasons—to glorify his name rather than our own. Positive changes in our thoughts, actions, and motives are the result of a changed nature.

Being and doing are different. Being suggests that one has internalized the teachings of Christ and is striving to become one of his followers. Being naturally results in doing. Conversely, doing alone suggests outward behaviors that may not result in the level of conversion required by true followers of Christ. Doing does not necessarily beget being.

The enemy to becoming or being is rationalizing. For many of us, especially those who have suffered from abuse, it's easy to rationalize our way into thinking we are Christlike and doing what is right. We are experts at going through the motions because of all the practice we had in the controlling environment at doing what was expected of us. However, when challenging situations arise as we reach adulthood, our world falls apart and we resort to survival mode, which may include but is not limited to such unhealthy patterns of behavior as perfectionism, anger toward others, rebellion against God, or even religious zealotry.

Christ said to the people in Israel, "Be ye therefore perfect, even as your Father which is in heaven is perfect" (Matthew 5:48). The standard for today's Christians is the same as it was in ancient days. That is, all who come unto Christ can be perfected in him as they deny themselves of all ungodliness and love God with all of their heart, might, mind, and strength (see Titus 2:12).

Unfortunately, the pattern of doing I've sometimes observed in myself and in others has less to do with being perfect and more to do with appearing perfect. The two can sometimes be confused.

The word *perfect* means to be spiritually reborn or to be whole. This process of becoming requires that we are meek and lowly of heart, repent of our sins, and submit our will to God's.

The Apostle Paul understood the difference between doing and being when he said:

> Though I speak with the tongues of men and of angels, and have not charity, I am become as sounding brass, or a tinkling cymbal. And though I have the gift of prophecy, and understand all mysteries,

and all knowledge; and though I have all faith, so that I could remove mountains, and have not charity, I am nothing. And though I bestow all my goods to feed the poor, and though I give my body to be burned, and have not charity, it profiteth me nothing. (1 Corinthians 13:1–3)

Paul then provides us with the following definition of charity:

Charity suffereth long, and is kind; charity envieth not; charity vaunteth not itself, is not puffed up, doth not behave itself unseemly, seeketh not her own, is not easily provoked, thinketh no evil; rejoiceth not in iniquity, but rejoiceth in the truth; beareth all things, believeth all things, hopeth all things, endureth all things. Charity never faileth: but whether there be prophecies, they shall fail; whether there be tongues, they shall cease; whether there be knowledge, it shall vanish away. (1 Corinthians 13:4–8)

Charity is the pure love of Christ. It includes receiving his great love for each of us and loving him. Charity is all about being more like him. We are children of a loving God. For he has sent his son to help show us the way to happiness in this life and the next.

CLINICAL INSIGHTS

THE JOURNEY

In time you'll learn that life is a process in which you learn, develop wisdom, and rise to a higher plane. You'll find that growing often hurts and change is sometimes painful, but that both growth and change are preferable to the alternatives.

It may seem that life is like drawing without an eraser in a world that requires constant correction. But you'll find that it's simply a journey that starts from where you are and moves only as fast as you're willing to go. Nevertheless, you won't learn that right away. It'll take a lot of falling down and getting up before you realize that you are the master of your fate.

You will have a tendency to compare yourself to others and to judge either yourself or someone else as a failure, but there are no failures. Some do, however, progress more slowly.

As you grow and develop with time and experience, a natural by-product of the journey will be either optimism or pessimism. Each is part of a pattern that develops in our perception, often without any real awareness on our part. It can go either way. Ultimately, it's the result of a choice you make every day.

In time, you'll learn that when you love life, life will love you back. You see, life is a self-fulfilling prophecy in which you won't get what you want, but you'll get what you expect. So learn to expect the best from yourself and not settle for mediocrity. For when you're mediocre, you're average, and when you're average, you're just as close to the bottom as you are to the top. Coming to understand such insight is a natural part of the journey.

In the midst of confusion and uncertainty, you'll tend to recognize the strength and wisdom that exist in other people. When this happens, seek to develop similar qualities in yourself but retain your unique individuality, for imitation of another is limitation of yourself. As you come to realize that some of your greatest teachers have been your own mistakes from which you have learned, you will find increased significance in the admonition to live your life as if your life depended on it—because it does.

PEACE OF MIND

To understand life is to live life more fully, but to be immobilized by confusion and anxiety is to slowly die. To appreciate who we really are is to discover our purpose in life, but to discredit ourselves is to sabotage our happiness.

To accept the truth that surrounds us is to free ourselves, but to misunderstand our limitations is to settle for bondage. To comprehend our strengths is to rise above our past, but to refuse to learn life's lessons is to repeat them.

To confront the problems that seek to destroy us is to create depth, but to mask the pain is to mismanage the learning opportunities.

To envision what we are capable of achieving is to design life, but to settle for mediocrity or allow anxiety to dictate our course is to destroy the purpose of our dreams.

To grasp the essence of our potential is to ennoble our efforts, but to misinterpret our weaknesses is to compromise their benefits. To face our fears is to overcome them, but to seek only to avoid them is to be controlled by them.

To anticipate success is to initiate a self-fulfilling prophesy, but to refuse to take necessary risks is to undermine our inherent worth. To learn from our mistakes is to invoke the powers of heaven, but to fail to learn from them is to cooperate with the powers of hell.

When you're stifled and stuck because of your fears and anxieties, remember the seven *R*s:

1. *Relabel the symptom.* Tell yourself, "It's not that bad." I can handle that. Then take charge of your thinking. No one ever dies of anxiety.

2. *Reattribute the symptom.* Remind yourself that it's anxiety and not you. Feelings are chemicals, and when there's a chemical imbalance, feelings get all mixed up. You're not mixed up.

3. *Refocus your attention.* Since you can't make the symptoms go away, decide to go on with the rest of your life in spite of them. Use relaxation techniques or try to focus on something more peaceful.

4. *Revalue the symptom.* The symptom is a message that something is out of balance. Once you understand that message, you can take steps to eliminate the symptom.

5. *Reprogram yourself.* Learn the basic tools and techniques to take care of yourself. Be optimistic and remember that you can only accomplish what you allow yourself to believe you can accomplish.

6. *Redefine yourself.* You are not your symptoms. You don't have to remain stuck beneath your symptoms. You can choose not to be a victim.

7. *Reframe your world.* Use your experiences. Learn from them, grow because of them, and progress as a result of them. Expand your comfort zones and reduce your expectations.

CONCLUSION

I N THIS LIFE, WE WILL EACH ENDURE VARIOUS TRIALS and tribulations. We have the power to choose how we will respond to these challenges. Whether we endure them well is ultimately up to each one of us.

Up to this point in my life, I haven't responded with faith and patience to many of life's challenges. In some ways, consciously or unconsciously, I believe I've used my experiences as a child as an excuse for not making much-needed changes. I now recognize that I've been greatly blessed throughout my life, and I'm acutely aware there are many others who have faced much greater challenges than I've ever had to endure.

In a Public Broadcasting System (PBS) documentary called *Return with Honor*, American prisoners of war were interviewed about their ordeal in North Vietnam prison camps. It was astounding to listen to these men as they spoke about being tortured, starved, and deprived in every imaginable way. Despite horrid conditions, these men spoke about how they chose to make the most of their difficult situation by keeping their minds and bodies active. When forced to endure torturous interrogations, they reminded themselves that they must be true to their country and return with honor at all costs. Some died under these harsh conditions. Others endured more than seven years in these camps before returning home.

I was touched by the faith and patience of these men. They could have easily chosen to remain bitter for the rest of their lives; instead, most of them commented that their experiences in the prison camps made them stronger, better people and brought them closer to God.

Most people desire to be happy, to love others, and to be loved. However, the effects of abuse or other unhealthy patterns of behavior may make it more challenging to experience these feelings. As we exercise faith in and hope of God's infinite capacity to bless our lives, we will discover that he truly loves us no matter how much we struggle to love ourselves. He will not forsake us as we strive to keep his commandments, remember him, and remember who we really are.

Although we may not fully understand why we must experience certain customized challenges, a loving God does understand. Life isn't fair as we perceive it; however, from an eternal perspective, mercy and justice will prevail!

My father passed away during the spring of 2011 at age eighty-four. Sadly, up until his death, he continued to treat my mother the same way he always treated her. He simply didn't appear to know how to act differently. Unfortunately, he chose not to seek the professional help required to successfully manage his mental health challenges.

I often wonder why my mother chose to endure so many years of abuse. I suppose one reason may be that she married at a young age. She was unable to complete her college education and develop marketable job skills. Another reason may be that her home environment made her feel she was helpless to survive without my father's financial support. Over the years, my siblings and I would encourage our mother to stick up for herself. However, like so many other individuals living under such circumstances, they fear what may happen to them or their children and don't seem to understand how to make the change. In fact, in most instances, they appear to resign themselves to defending the abusers and wonder why others can't see their many good qualities as well. The third reason my mother stayed with my father may be that she loved him. Despite his mental health issues and the personal struggles they endured together for more than sixty years, perhaps she hoped that someday he too would be healed and they could enjoy a loving relationship free from the consequences of his mental illness.

In the end, we all have a choice! We can choose to live in a world of darkness and despair or choose a better way. For many of us, choosing a better way includes doing what is necessary to heal emotionally and grow spiritually. If we don't, many of life's challenges may force us into reorganizing the way we look at the world and cause us to leave our old comfort zones regardless. Eventually, we learn to think outside the box in terms of perception and personal expectations and to recognize that we don't need to be defined by our weaknesses, our family dysfunctions, or our culture. We can begin to understand that we're part of something much bigger than we may have previously understood.

May we earnestly strive to recognize God's hand in our lives and realize there is reason to rejoice! We have the teachings of Jesus Christ and the blessings of his infinite atonement, which can help bring hope and healing, strengthen our faith, and enable us to experience God's great love for each of us.

CLINICAL INSIGHTS

The problems we encounter in life and the pain that results from them enable us to discover a variety of unique personal characteristics, the accumulation of which helps us to define both ourselves and the world around us. Because this is a dynamic process in which everything is always in transition, it is clear we can be either the architect of our perception or the victim of it.

I've come to believe that most of us will behave maturely, logically, and rationally in life, but not until we have exhausted every other alternative. In this process, we choose to be happy or not. Simply put, being happy and healthy means recognizing that we're ultimately in charge of our lives and that we're responsible for the choices we make. Unhealthy thinking patterns indicate that we have no choices. When we practice being unhealthy, we usually find ourselves running from and confronted by the very things we were trying to avoid.

Unfortunately, sometimes we become so unhealthy that we become disconnected from ourselves, from our feelings, and from our strengths; disconnected from the love and support of others; and disconnected from God and from the ultimate source of healing and strength. When we're disconnected, we have only our own resources to draw from. When our well goes dry, which invariably it will, it can be terrifying.

Ironically, in spite of these problems, we become highly resistant to making any changes—even when it is clear that the course we're on is filled with pain and confusion. As we continue the behaviors that keep us on this self-defeating course, our fears will imprison us. The belief that someone else controls the cell door and that we can never open it paralyzes us. In reality, the door was never locked.

Life should be filled with experiences and growth, not indecision, hesitation, or excuses. But when emotional paralysis settles in with a stranglehold that distorts perception, there is no opportunity to gain the inspiration and emancipation that comes from overcoming the conditions of mortality. Both our strengths and weaknesses are developed by the manner in which we face these conditions. In essence, they make us different, and different is good.

Our experiences and unique conditions help to define who we really are. Nothing of any consequence can be achieved without overcoming opposition, and overcoming opposition requires discipline and commitment. These are the fundamental principles that allow each of us to overcome our previous state.

Unfortunately, we often fail to understand that we are now in the process of becoming what we will be. When applied to the development of skills and abilities, becoming is often viewed as a painful process, brilliantly disguised as being a task that is almost impossible to achieve. Some people hesitate, seeing only the pain. Others become empowered and strengthened, recognizing the pain only as a façade of apparent impossibility.

In reality, our problems are the necessary ingredients that allow each of us to be tried and tested, tempered and forged. Only by confronting our problems will we be able to realize the inherent potential with which each of us has been endowed.

On his epic voyage to the New World, Christopher Columbus experienced one problem after another. Even though this opposition challenged both his sanity and his ability, he fulfilled his destiny as he remained true to his dream. He understood that it was impossible to discover distant places without having the courage to lose sight of his own familiar shore. More important, he understood principles of even greater significance—discipline, commitment, and perseverance. In spite of all the problems, fears, and challenges he faced, he kept his focus on the distant horizon because he was determined to succeed. And day after day in his ship's log, he entered only these words, "This day we sailed on."

The poet John Greenleaf Whittier wrote, "For all sad words of tongue and pen, the saddest are these, 'it might have been.'"[1] We can't afford to let these words be our epitaph. Let the redefining process begin now!

Redefining ourselves means redesigning and rebuilding ourselves with all of the wisdom and insight that we've gained from making the mistakes of the past. It means rebounding from the pain, reversing the negative thinking, and remembering who we are—children of God. It means remaining constant under pressure, recovering when we fall, resisting old patterns, recommitting ourselves to higher principles, and reminding ourselves that our worth is unconditional.

In essence, redefining ourselves is the first step toward moving in a new direction. It includes letting go of past hurts and relationships that destroy our progress. This new direction allows us to experience a change of heart, feel increased love for God, others, and ourselves; and to see things as they really are—full of light, color, and beauty.

Like a beautiful butterfly that emerges from its cocoon, we too can experience the same miraculous transformation; one that will change our lives in many wonderful ways. As we undergo this transformation, we'll find there are those who are not ready for us to change. They may be uncomfortable with the new person we're becoming and intentionally or unintentionally attempt to treat us the way that we were before. As we remain strong during this process of inner change, exercising faith and patience along the way, we'll soon discover that the people around us also have choices. They too can choose a path that leads them to experience the same miraculous transformation, or they can choose to move in a different direction. In the end, it's all about the choices we make.

NOTES

1. John Greenleaf Whittier, accessed December 12, 2011, http://thinkexist.com/quote/John_Greenleaf_Whittier.

ONLINE MENTAL HEALTH RESOURCES AND INFORMATION

Anxiety Disorders Association of America (ADAA)

http://www.adaa.org

The ADAA is a national nonprofit organization dedicated to the prevention, treatment, and cure of anxiety disorders and to improving the lives of all people who suffer from them.

Children and Adults with Attention Deficit Disorders (CHADD)

http://www.chadd.org

CHADD is a national nonprofit organization providing education, advocacy, and support for individuals with ADD.

Edward G. Callister Foundation

http://www.hopetoday.com

The purpose of the Edward G. Callister Foundation is to help increase public awareness of the individual, family, and societal problems associated with substance abuse.

National Alliance for Mental Illness (NAMI)

http://www.nami.org

NAMI is a resource for families struggling with mental illness issues. Links cover current legislation at the national level, fact sheets, and a variety of excellent programs from NAMI.

National Mental Health Information Center

http://mentalhealth.samhsa.gov

This substance abuse and mental health site contains information about promising practices for children and youth mental health. It focuses on the need for interagency, community-wide coordination, and support for children and families.

Obsessive-Compulsive Foundation

http://www.ocfoundation.org

The OC Foundation is committed to finding and promoting effective treatment for individuals with obsessive-compulsive disorders.

School Mental Health

www.schoolmentalhealth.org

This website offers practical and easy–to-access mental health resources for clinicians, educators, families, and students. Resources provided offer information on best practices in school mental health and have a particular focus on advancing evidence-based practice.

The National Institute of Mental Health (NIMH)

http://www.nimh.nih.gov

NIMH is the largest scientific organization in the world dedicated to research focused on the understanding, treatment, and prevention of mental disorders and the promotion of mental health.

INDEX

ABOUT THE AUTHORS

L OWELL K. OSWALD WAS born in Rexburg, Idaho, and raised in Utah. He has spent over thirty years developing services and programs for at-risk children and youth. Lowell has been employed as a high school teacher, educational diagnostician, school district administrator, and state personnel development director. He is passionate about improving the educational and mental health services for students struggling with emotional and behavior disorders, and has devoted most of his life to serving this population. Lowell obtained a bachelor's degree at the University of Utah, a master's degree at Utah State University, and a PhD at the University of Utah. He also completed two years of post-doctoral work in the school psychology program at the University of Utah. Lowell and his wife, Laurie, have been married for thirty-one years. They have three children and one grandchild.

JOHN WATERBURY WAS born in Guelph, Ontario, Canada, and raised in Illinois. He was nominated for the Marty Mann Award for a series of radio vignettes on alcoholism and wrote a popular weekly newspaper column that was widely read in Kentucky, Texas, Utah, and Tennessee. John attended Arkansas State University, where he received bachelor's and master's degrees. He is a licensed professional counselor and national certified counselor. John was a frequent guest on a daily radio talk show and presents workshops on topics related to mental illness and abuse. He also taught at the University of Tennessee. John and his wife, Melinda, have been married for forty years. They have four children and ten grandchildren.